19.4.60

הנדון : סימני זהרת והיכר של חם

סיסמך
9.7.37

יולי 1937

ס"מ 56
41

בנוסף למצוייך ברשימה המצ"ב ישבם סימצים נוספים שאותם פרסמתי ותמ.

א. תאור צורת הדיבור, ניב הדיבור, מבנה גוף כללי, שפ (בין היתר עברית) רכו' . המצויינים בעדותו של ריסל משנת 1946.

ב. מס' ב- 45326 S.S (יתכן וזה היה מקועקע?)
מס' במפלגה 889895.
מס' ב- S.S. -6.375ZA (לא ידוע לנו פירוש מספר זה)
פרסים אלו מקרום במסמכי S.S, משנת 1932 ו-1937.

ב ב ר כ ה

THE NAZI H

Scholastic Inc.

UNTERS

NEAL BASCOMB

To Justice Served

— N.B.

....

Copyright © 2013 by Neal Bascomb

For photo credits, see page 239.

Arthur A. Levine Books hardcover edition designed by Phil
Falco, published by Arthur A. Levine Books, an imprint of
Scholastic Inc., September 2013.

ISBN 978-0-545-43100-2

10 9 8 7 6 5 4 3   19 20 21 22

Printed in the U.S.A. 23

This edition first printing 2018

Book design by Phil Falco

....

EICHMANN FAMILY

Adolf Eichmann, Nazi commander in charge of
  transportation for the Final Solution

Vera Eichmann, his wife

Nikolas (Klaus, Nick), Horst, Dieter, and Ricardo
  Eichmann, his sons

AUSCHWITZ SURVIVOR

Zeev Sapir

NAZI HUNTERS

Fritz Bauer, District Attorney of the West
  German state of Hesse

Manus Diamant

Lothar Hermann

Sylvia Hermann

Simon Wiesenthal

ISRAELI DEFENSE FORCES

Zvi Aharoni, chief interrogator for the Shin Bet,
  the Israeli internal security service

Shalom Dani, forgery expert

Rafi Eitan, Shin Bet Chief of Operations

Yonah Elian, civilian doctor

Yaakov Gat, agent for the Mossad, the Israeli secret
  intelligence network

Yoel Goren, Mossad agent

Isser Harel, head of the Mossad

Ephraim Hofstetter, head of criminal investigations
  at the Tel Aviv police

Ephraim Ilani, Mossad agent, based out of the
  Israeli embassy in Argentina
Peter Malkin, Shin Bet agent
Yaakov Medad, Mossad agent
Avraham Shalom, Deputy Head of Operations for
  Shin Bet
Moshe Tabor, Mossad agent

EL AL PERSONNEL - AIRLINE MANAGEMENT
Yosef Klein, Manager of El Al's base at Idlewild
  Airport in New York City
Adi Peleg, Head of Security
Yehuda Shimoni, Manager
Baruch Tirosh, Head of Crew Assignments

EL AL PERSONNEL - FLIGHT CREW
Shimon Blanc, engineer
Gady Hassin, navigator
Oved Kabiri, engineer
Azriel Ronen, copilot
Shaul Shaul, navigator
Zvi Tohar, captain
Shmuel Wedeles, copilot

OTHER ISRAELIS
David Ben-Gurion, first Prime Minister of Israel
Haim Cohen, Attorney General of Israel
Gideon Hausner, Second Attorney General of Israel

"Justice should not only be done,
but should manifestly and undoubtedly
be seen to be done."
—Lord Chief Justice Gordon Hewart, 1924

"I sat at my desk and did my work. It
was my job to catch our Jewish enemies like
fish in a net and transport them to
their final destination."

—Adolf Eichmann

"We will bring Adolf Eichmann to
Jerusalem, and perhaps the world will
be reminded of its responsibilities."

—Isser Harel

PROLOGUE

A remote stretch of unlit road on a windy night. Two cars appear out of the darkness. One of them, a Chevrolet, slows to a halt, and its headlights blink off. The Buick drives some distance farther, then turns onto Garibaldi Street, where it too stops and its lights turn off. Two men climb out of the back of the Buick and walk to the front of the car, where one lifts the hood. Their breath steams in the cold air. One leans his burly frame over the engine. Another man gets out of the front passenger seat and climbs into the back, shutting the door after him. His forehead presses against the cold glass; his eyes fix on the highway and the bus stop.

In five minutes, the bus will arrive. There is no reason for any of the men to speak. They have only to wait and to watch.

A train roars across the bridge that spans the highway.

A young man wearing a bright red jacket, about fifteen years old, pedals down Garibaldi Street on his bicycle. He notices the Buick and stops to ask if they need any help. It's a remote neighborhood with few houses, after all. The driver steps halfway out of the car and, smiling at the youth, says in Spanish, "Thank you! No need! You can carry on your way."

The men standing outside the car smile and wave at the youth too but stay silent. He takes off, his unzipped jacket flapping around him in the wind. There is a storm on the way.

Suddenly, headlights split the darkness. The green and yellow municipal bus emerges, but instead of stopping at exactly 7:44 P.M., as it has done every other night the men have kept watch, it keeps going. It rattles past the Chevrolet, underneath the railway bridge, and then it is gone.

The man in the back of the Buick limousine speaks briefly. "We stay," he insists. Nobody argues.

At 8:05, they see a faint halo of light in the distance. Another bus's headlights shine brightly down the highway. This one slows and stops. Brakes screech, the door clatters open, and two passengers step out. As the bus pulls away, one of them, a woman, turns to the left, while the other, a man, heads for Garibaldi Street. He bends forward into the wind, his hands stuffed in his coat pockets.

He has no idea what is waiting for him.

CHAPTER 1

Lieutenant Colonel Adolf Eichmann stood at the head of the convoy of 140 military vehicles. It was noon on Sunday, March 19, 1944, his thirty-eighth birthday. He held his trim frame stiff, leaning slightly forward as he watched his men prepare to move out.

The engines rumbled to life, and black exhaust spewed across the road. Eichmann climbed into his Mercedes staff car and signaled for the motorcycle troops to lead the way.

More than five hundred members of the Schutzstaffel, the Nazi security service — better known as the SS — were in the convoy, leaving Mauthausen, a concentration camp in Austria, for Budapest, Hungary. Their mission was to comb Hungary from east to west and find all of the country's 750,000 Jews. Anyone who was physically fit was to be delivered to the labor camps for "destruction through work"; anyone who was not was to be immediately killed.

Eichmann had planned it all carefully. He had been in charge of Jewish affairs for the Nazis for eight years and was now chief of Department IVB_4, responsible for executing Hitler's policy to wipe out the Jews. He ran his office like it was a business, setting clear, ambitious targets, recruiting efficient staff members and delegating to them, and traveling frequently to monitor their progress. He measured his success not in battles won but in schedules met, quotas filled, and units moved. In Austria,

Adolf Eichmann in uniform during World War II.

Germany, France, Italy, the Netherlands, Belgium, Denmark, Slovakia, Romania, and Poland, Eichmann had perfected his methods. Now it was Hungary's turn.

Stage one was to isolate the Jews. They would be ordered to wear Yellow Star emblems on their clothes, forbidden to travel or to use phones and radios, and banned from scores of professions. He would remove them from Hungarian society.

Stage two would secure Jewish wealth for the Third Reich. Factories and businesses would be taken over, bank accounts would be frozen, and the assets of every single individual would be seized, down to their ration cards.

Stage three: the ghettos. Jews would be uprooted from their homes and sent to live in concentrated, miserable neighborhoods until the fourth and final stage could be effected: the camps. As soon as the Jews arrived at those, another SS department would be responsible for their fate. They would no longer be Adolf Eichmann's concern. That was how he saw it.

To prevent escapes or uprisings, Eichmann planned to deceive the Jewish community leaders. He would meet them face to face and promise them that the restrictions were only temporary, the necessities of Germany's war with the Allies, which had been going on for four and a half years. As long as the leaders cooperated, he would reassure them, no harm would come to them or to their community. He might take a few bribes as well. Not only would the money add even more Jewish wealth to the German haul, he would also fool more Jews into thinking they might save themselves if they could pay up. Even when they were forced onto the trains to the camps, the Jews would be told either that they were being moved for their own safety or that they were going to supply labor for Germany.

Eichmann knew that these deceptions would buy time and acquiescence. Brute force would do the rest. He thought it best to initiate stages three and four in the more remote districts of Hungary first, and to leave the capital, Budapest, for last.

• • •

At dawn on April 15, the last day of Passover, gendarmes came to Zeev Sapir's door in the village of Dobradovo. They were from the Hungarian police, which was cooperating with the occupying German troops. Zeev was twenty years old and lived with his parents and five younger siblings. The gendarmes woke up the family and ordered them to pack. They could bring food, clothes, and bedding — no more than fifty kilograms per person. The few valuable family heirlooms they owned were confiscated.

The gendarmes bullied and whipped everyone in the community — 103 people — to the nearby town of Munkács. The very young and the very old were brought in horse-drawn hay carts. They reached Munkács in the evening, exhausted from carrying their baggage. Over the next several days, 14,000 Jews from the city and surrounding regions crammed into the old Munkács brick factory and its grounds. They were told that they had been removed from the "military operational zone" to protect them from the advancing Russians.

This news was no comfort to Zeev. His family now lived on the factory grounds, in a shelter with a roof but no walls, and with little food apart from spoonfuls of potato soup. There was hardly any water — only two faucets for the whole ghetto. The Hungarian gendarmes played cruel games with them, forcing work gangs to transfer piles of bricks from one end of the brickyard to the other for no reason other than to exercise their power.

Hungarian gendarmes guard the entrance to the Munkács ghetto.

As the days and nights passed, the crying of hungry and thirsty children became almost too much for Zeev to bear.

Then came the rains. There was no escaping the downpour that turned the brickyards into a mud pit and brought on epidemics of typhoid and pneumonia. Somehow, Zeev, his parents, his four younger brothers (ages fifteen, eleven, six, and three), and his sister (age eight) avoided getting sick.

After three weeks in the ghetto, Zeev heard that there would be a visit from a high-ranking SS officer. Perhaps this "Eichmann" would be able to tell them what was going to happen to them.

When Adolf Eichmann arrived, the entire population of the ghetto was forcibly assembled in the main yard. Flanked by thirty Hungarian and SS officers, Eichmann strode into the camp in his polished black boots. He announced to the prisoners, "Jews: You have nothing to worry about. We want only the best for you. You'll leave here shortly and be sent to very fine places indeed. You will work there, your wives will stay at home, and your children will go to school. You will have wonderful lives."

Zeev had no choice but to believe him.

Soon after Eichmann's visit, the trains arrived. Brandishing whips, blackjacks, and tommy guns, guards forced everyone into the rail yard. Every last man, woman, and child was stripped, their clothes and few belongings searched for any remaining valuables. Those reluctant to follow orders were beaten. Terror and confusion reigned.

A guard tore Zeev's personal documents into shreds and then gave him back his clothes. Then all 103 Dobradovo Jews, including Zeev and his family, were crammed into a train car meant for eight cows. There was a bucket of water to drink and an empty bucket for a toilet. The guards slammed the

Jews are crowded into a cattle car and brought through France.

door shut, casting them into darkness, and then padlocked the door.

The train rattled to a start. Nobody knew where they were going. Someone tried to read the platform signs of the small railway stations they passed to get an idea of their direction, but it was too difficult to see through the carriage's small window, which was strung with barbed wire to prevent escape.

By the end of the first day, the heat, stench, hunger, and thirst had become unbearable. The Sapir children wept for water and something to eat; Zeev's mother soothed them with whispers of "Go to sleep, my child." Zeev stood most of the time. There was little room to sit, and that was reserved for the weakest. Villagers of all ages fainted from exhaustion; several died from suffocation. At one point, the train halted at a station. The door opened, and a guard asked if they wanted water. Zeev scrambled out to fill the bucket. Just as he arrived back, the guard knocked the brimming bucket from his hands and the water seeped away into the ground.

Four days after leaving Munkács, the train came to a screeching stop. It was late at night, and when the door crashed open, searchlights burned the passengers' eyes. SS guards shouted, "Out! Get out! Quick!" Dogs barked as the Jews poured from the train, even more emaciated than they had been before. A shop owner from Dobradovo turned back: He had left his prayer shawl in the train. A prisoner in a striped uniform, who was carrying away their baggage, asked, "What do you need your prayer shawl for? Soon you'll be going there." He pointed toward a chimney belching smoke.

They had arrived at Auschwitz.

An officer divided the new arrivals into two lines with a flick

Hungarian Jews from the Tet ghetto arrive at Auschwitz, May 27, 1944.

of his hand or a sharp "left" or "right." Zeev was directed to the left, his parents and siblings to the right. He struggled to stay with them but was beaten back by the guards.

He never saw his family again.

• • •

Adolf Eichmann had not reckoned that the war with the Allies would interfere with his plans to exterminate the Jews, but on July 2, 1944, six weeks after his arrival in Budapest, air-raid sirens wailed throughout the city. At 8:30 A.M., the first of 750 Allied heavy bombers, led by the U.S. Fifteenth Air

Force, released its explosives. Antiaircraft guns and German fighter planes attempted to defend Budapest against the surprise attack, but they were overwhelmed by wave after wave of bombs.

When the bombardment was over, Eichmann emerged from his hilltop villa — a fine two-story building formerly owned by a Jewish industrialist — to find Allied propaganda leaflets drifting down from the sky onto his lawn. They said that the Soviets were pushing east through Romania, and that the Allies had landed in France and Italy and were driving toward Germany. The Third Reich was facing defeat, the leaflets declared, and all resistance should cease. President Franklin Roosevelt insisted that the persecution of Hungarian Jews and other minorities must stop. Those responsible would be hunted down and punished.

Eichmann was unmoved. He had traveled a long road to become who he was, the man who sent millions of Jews to their deaths. Born in an industrial town in Germany, he had been raised in Linz, Austria, by a father who was a middle-class manager, a strict Protestant, and an ardent nationalist. Eichmann joined the Nazi Party in 1932, when he was twenty-five. He was a handsome young man, with fine, dark-blond hair, narrow lips, a long nose, and grayish-blue eyes. He went to Germany, received some military training, and enlisted in the Sicherheitsdienst (SD), the Nazi intelligence service. Diligent, attentive to detail, and respectful of authority, he caught the eye of the man in charge of creating a Jewish affairs office. Given the degree of revulsion Hitler felt toward the Jewish people, Eichmann knew that being part of that office would serve his career well. Beginning in 1935, he spent three years studying the German

Obersturmbannführer Adolf Eichmann of the SS, with top Nazi brass.

Jews and formulating plans to move them to Palestine — the preferred Nazi answer to "the Jewish question" at the time.

The more territory the Nazis occupied, the more Jews came under their control, which meant more responsibilities and opportunities for Eichmann. When Germany seized Poland in September 1939, Heinrich Müller, the new chief of the German secret police, the Gestapo, gave Eichmann the job of running the Central Office for Jewish Emigration. Their new goal was to deport Jews to the edges of German-occupied territory to make room for ethnic Germans. Eichmann even came up with a plan to resettle millions of Jews in Madagascar, off the southeast coast of Africa, although this never came to pass.

In late summer 1941, Reinhard Heydrich, the head of the Nazi spy service, summoned Eichmann to Berlin and told him, "The Führer has ordered physical extermination." Eichmann was sent to report on killing operations already under way in Poland. He saw death squads organized by Heydrich follow the German army into Eastern Europe and Russia and set to work murdering Jews, Gypsies, Communists, and any other "enemies" of the Reich. Near Lodz, Poland, men, women, and children were rounded up and loaded into vans that were pumped full of exhaust fumes, poisoning everyone inside. In the Ukraine, people were forced into pits, ordered to strip, and then shot in the hundreds.

Despite his feelings toward Jews, Eichmann was unnerved by what he saw. But the fear of losing his job, and the power that went with it, outweighed his misgivings, and he accepted the need to rid Europe of the Jews through extermination. Though only a lieutenant colonel, Eichmann was appointed head of Department IVB_4, the SS division responsible for the Jews, in charge of managing all matters related to "the Final Solution of the Jewish question," as Adolf Hitler called it.

Eichmann took on his new job with bloodless enthusiasm. He got rid of any guilt and discomfort by telling himself that his bosses had "given their orders." He had not set the policy of annihilation, he reasoned, but it was his responsibility to make sure it was a success. The more Jews he brought to the extermination camps, the better he looked to his superiors and the better he served the Reich. And in this he excelled, delivering millions to their deaths.

With each challenge, with each victory, he grew a little more obsessive about his work, a little more convinced of its

Der Chef der Sicherheitspolizei und des SD

Berlin SW 11, den 11. März 194.
Prinz-Albrecht-Straße 8
Fernsprecher: 12 00 40

IV B 4 a   3233/42g(NH)

Geheim

Schnellbrief

Auswärtiges Amt
pol. III 250. g
Eing. 12. MRZ. 1942
Rcl. (lsa) Bem. b. Eing.

An das

Auswärtige Amt,
z.Hдn. von Herrn Legationsrat R a d e m a c h e r ,

B e r l i n W 35,

Rauchstrasse 11.

Betrifft: Evakuierung von Juden aus Frankreich.
Bezug: Hies.Schnellbrief vom 9.3.42
          - IV B 4 a - 3233/41g (1550) -

       Im Nachgang zum hiesigen Schnell-
brief vom 9.3.1942 wird mitgeteilt, daß außer
der am 23.3.1942 vorgesehenen Evakuierung von
1.000 Juden aus Compiègne in Zeitkürze weitere
5.000 staatspolizeilich in Erscheinung getre-
tene Juden aus Frankreich in das Konzentra-
tionslager Auschwitz (Oberschlesien) abgescho-
ben werden sollen.

       Ich darf bitten, auch hierzu die
dortige Zustimmung auszusprechen.

                    Im Auftrage:

                    Eichmann

261430

With this letter, dated March 11, 1942, Eichmann ordered the
deportation of six thousand Jews from France to Auschwitz.

importance, and a little more drawn to the power he held over life and death. Jews were no longer human beings, no longer even units to be moved from one place to another. Jews were a disease. "They were stealing the breath of life from us," he wrote.

In August 1944, with the war going poorly for Germany, the Nazi leadership came to see the Jews as much-needed bargaining chips. Eichmann thought that this was weakness. When the Russians took Romania, Heinrich Himmler, who was in charge of the entire Final Solution, shelved the plans for Jewish deportation, and Eichmann was ordered to disband his unit. He refused. Neither an Allied bombing nor a threat by an American president nor even Hitler himself was going to divert him from completing his masterpiece: the destruction of Hungarian Jewry. The Jews needed to be eradicated, and Eichmann was the one who would see it through to the end.

He stayed in Budapest, waiting for his chance to get back to work. He dined at fashionable restaurants and drank himself into a stupor at cabarets. While away from his wife, Vera, and their three sons, he had two steady mistresses: one a rich, thirty-year-old divorcée, the other the consort of a Hungarian count. He went horse-riding and took his jeep out to the countryside. He spent weekends at castles or just stayed in his villa, with its lavish gardens and retinue of servants.

In late October, with the Russians only a hundred miles from the city, Eichmann made one last bid to finish what he had started. "You see, I'm back again," he declared to the capital's Jewish leaders. There were no trains to take the Jews the 125 miles to the labor camps in Austria because of the bombing raids, so Eichmann sent twenty-seven thousand people, including children and the sick, off on foot.

With few provisions and no shelter, the weak soon began falling behind. They were either shot or left to die in roadside ditches. It was intentional slaughter, something that Himmler had ordered must now stop. Yet even when Eichmann was given a direct order by a superior officer to call off the march, he ignored it.

At last, in early December, Himmler himself summoned Eichmann to his headquarters in the Black Forest of Germany. "If until now you have killed Jews," he told Eichmann, in a tone laced with anger, "from now on, I order you, you must be a fosterer of Jews. . . . If you are not able to do that, you must tell me so!"

"Yes, Reichsführer," Eichmann answered obediently.

• • •

When Zeev Sapir arrived in Auschwitz in May 1944, he was beaten, stripped, deloused, shaved, and tattooed with a number on his left forearm: A3800. The next morning he was forced to work in the gas chambers, where he suspected his family had been killed the previous day. Zeev dragged out the dead and placed them on their backs in the yard, where a barber cut off their hair and a dental mechanic ripped out any gold teeth. Then he carried the corpses to large pits, where they were stacked like logs and burned to ashes. A channel running through the middle of the pit drained the fat from the bodies — fat that was then used to fuel the crematorium fires. The smoke was thick, the flames dark red.

As the months passed, Zeev lost track of time. He never knew what day of the week it was, or even what hour of the day. The Germans regularly killed workers like him so as to keep their activities secret. Somehow he escaped execution. Eventually, he was sent to Jaworzno, a satellite camp of Auschwitz, where he went to work in the Dachsgrube coal mines. He had to fill forty-five wagons of coal every twelve-hour shift or receive twenty-five lashes. He often fell short.

Then it was winter. Curled into a ball on his bunk one morning, Zeev could not stop shivering. The December wind whistled through the gaps in the hut's walls. He had swapped his spare shirt for a loaf of bread, and his clothes hung loosely in rags on his skeletal body. At 4:30 A.M., a siren sounded, and Zeev leapt down from his bunk. He hurried outside with the hundred other prisoners from his hut, completely exposed now to the bitter wind, and they marched off to the mines.

When Zeev returned to the camp that evening, bone weary and coated with coal dust, he and the other three thousand prisoners

Jewish laborers are forced to work in a mine near Lodz, Poland.

were ordered back out on a march. The Red Army was advancing into Poland, the SS guards told them. Zeev did not much care. He was told to walk, so he would walk. That attitude — and a lot of luck — had kept him alive for eight months.

They trudged through deep snow for two days, not knowing where they were going. Anyone who slowed down or stopped for a rest was shot dead. As night fell on the second day, they reached Bethune, a town in eastern Poland, and were told to sit by the side of the road. The commanding officer strode down the line, saying, "Whoever is unable to continue may remain here, and he will be transferred by truck." Zeev had learned not to believe such promises, but he was too tired, too cold, and too indifferent to care. He and two hundred other prisoners stayed put while the rest marched away.

Zeev slept where he had fallen in the snow. In the morning, his group was ordered out to a field with shovels and pickaxes and told to dig. The earth was frozen, but they dug and dug, even though they knew they were digging their own graves.

That evening, they were taken to the dining hall at a nearby mine. All the windows had been blown out by air raids. A number of SS officers followed them inside, led by a deputy officer named Lausmann. "Yes, I know you are so hungry," he said in a sympathetic tone as a large pot was brought into the hall.

The most desperate pushed to the front, hoping for food. Lausmann grabbed one of them, leaned him over the pot, and shot him in the neck. Then he reached for the next one. He fired and fired. One young prisoner began making a speech to anyone who would listen. "The German people will answer to history for this," he declared. Then he received a bullet as well.

Lausmann continued to fire until there were only eleven

prisoners left, Zeev among them. Before he could be summoned forward, Lausmann was called away by his superior officer. He did not return. The guards took the remaining prisoners by train to the Gleiwitz concentration camp, where they were thrown into a cellar filled with potatoes. Starving, they ate the frozen, raw potatoes.

The next morning, with thousands of others, they were marched out to the forest. Suddenly, machine guns opened fire on them. Zeev ran through the trees until his legs gave out. His fall knocked him unconscious. He woke up alone, with a bloody foot and only one shoe. When the Russian army found him later that day, he weighed sixty-four pounds. His skin was as yellow and dry as parchment. It was January 1945, and he would not regain anything close to physical health until April.

Zeev Sapir never forgot the promise Eichmann made in the Munkács ghetto or the call to justice by his fellow prisoner the moment before his execution. But many, many years would pass before he was brought forward to remember these things.

• • •

In the few remaining hours before the Allies' final attack on Berlin in April 1945, Adolf Eichmann returned to his German office and gathered his dejected unit together. He bid them good-bye, saying that he knew the war was lost and that they should do what they could to stay alive. Then he said, "I will gladly and happily jump into the pit with the knowledge that with me are 5 million enemies of the Reich." Five million was the number of Jews Eichmann estimated had been killed in his Holocaust.

On May 2, he went to the lakeside village of Altaussee, Austria, in the narrow wooded valley at the foot of the Dachstein and Totengebirge mountains, where he met up with his family. The village was teeming with Nazi Party leaders and members of the Gestapo. A few days later, an orderly arrived with a directive from Himmler: "It is prohibited to fire on Englishmen and Americans." The war was over.

Eichmann knew that the Allies would brand him a war criminal, and he was determined to avoid capture. He said good-bye to his wife, Vera, and told her that he would contact her again when he had settled somewhere safe. Then he went out to the lake, where his sons — Nikolas (who was known as Klaus and who was nine years old), Horst (five), and Dieter (three) — were playing. Little Dieter slipped and fell into the lake. Eichmann fished his son out of the water, took him over his knee, and slapped him hard several times. Over Dieter's yells, Eichmann shouted at him not to go near the water. He might never see his boys again, he thought; it was best to leave them with a bit of discipline. Then he embraced them in turn.

"Be brave and look after the children," he told Vera.

As he hiked away into the mountains, Eichmann was far from prepared to be a man on the run. He had little money, no safe house, and no forged papers. Unlike some of his SS comrades, he had not salted away a fortune in gold and foreign currency. Now he regretted that he had not kept the bribes he took from the Jewish leaders, who would have given him everything they had in exchange for their lives.

CHAPTER 2

"Have you heard of Adolf Eichmann?" asked a captain of the Jewish Brigade, a British army unit.

"I heard the name from some Hungarian Jews at Mauthausen," Simon Wiesenthal said. "It means nothing to me."

"Better look it up," the captain replied.

It was mid-June 1945. Only four weeks earlier, weighing ninety-seven pounds, Wiesenthal had staggered out of a barracks at the Mauthausen concentration camp to see a gray American tank coming through the entrance. He had collapsed at the sight.

Before the Nazis stormed into Poland, Wiesenthal had been an architect with a rising reputation and a husband with hopes for a family of his own. The Nazis had killed his mother and taken his wife, and he had suffered such terror on his body and mind that he had twice attempted to kill himself.

After his liberation, Wiesenthal was afraid that if he did not go after those responsible for the slaughter, he would have nothing to live for. He sent a letter to the chief investigator of an American army war-crimes unit, chronicling the twelve concentration camps he had survived and listing the names, ranks, and crimes of ninety-one Nazis. The investigator hired him immediately. Wiesenthal captured more than a dozen SS members with the army unit before he was transferred to the American Office of Strategic Services (OSS), based in Linz, Austria.

Simon Wiesenthal in the 1960s.

Now Wiesenthal searched through the files at the OSS headquarters. There was limited information on Eichmann, but he noted the name so that he could make future inquiries. In the month that followed, he heard little more than rumors about Eichmann from former Mauthausen inmates. Then, in late July, he was given a list of war criminals' names by the Jewish Agency for Palestine (a forerunner of the Israeli government). The name Eichmann topped the list, stating that he was a "high official of Gestapo headquarters, Department of Jewish Affairs." Wiesenthal knew that this meant Eichmann had been instrumental in running the extermination camps.

A few evenings later, at his apartment on Landstrasse 40, just two doors down from the OSS office in Linz, Wiesenthal sat at his desk, looking at his own list of names. *Eichmann* was now underscored for emphasis.

His landlady entered to clean his room and peered over his shoulder. "Eichmann!" she exclaimed. "That must be the SS general Eichmann who was in command of the Jews. Did you know his parents live here in this street? Just a few houses along, at number 32."

On July 28, two OSS agents were at the elder Eichmanns' door. They questioned Eichmann's father, who reluctantly admitted that his son Adolf had been a member of the SS, but that was all he knew of his wartime activities. Adolf had visited near the end of the war, but his father had heard nothing from him since. A search of the house failed to deliver a single photograph. "Is there a picture?" one of them asked, suspicious that the man was hiding something.

"He never liked to be photographed," answered Eichmann's father.

● ● ●

The Nazi hunters were on Eichmann's trail, and finding a photograph for identification purposes was high on their list. In 1947, Jewish agent Manus Diamant was given the task. Handsome as a movie star, and with all the charm of one, Diamant could play any undercover role with ease. Using the story that he was a former Dutch SS officer by the name of Henry van Diamant, he earned the confidence of Eichmann's wife, Vera, who was still living in Altaussee, and he wooed several of Eichmann's mistresses in his efforts to gather information.

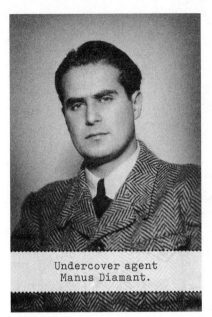
Undercover agent
Manus Diamant.

Vera Eichmann was very guarded and offered no hint of her husband's whereabouts — or even whether he was alive. None of Eichmann's mistresses had as much as a snapshot of him. Then Diamant tracked down Fräulein Maria Mösenbacher. An attractive, frivolous woman, Mösenbacher often bragged of her relationship with "Adolf," the high-ranking SS officer. For a week Diamant followed her, noting when she went to the hairdresser, the grocer, and the post office. When some groceries fell from her basket one day, he was there to pick them up. He introduced himself with a smile. "Henry van Diamant."

"Thank you. Thank you very much. My name is Maria . . . Thank you." Diamant tipped his hat and offered to walk her home. Over the next few weeks, he gained her trust. They met for coffee, then dinner, then a walk in the country. One evening, he deliberately let his wallet fall open to show his forged Dutch SS identification. He bought her blouses and chocolates. To convince her of his interest in photography, he gave her some landscape shots he said he had taken himself but which he had in fact bought.

Then, one night, a few weeks after they had met, he brought an album of "family photos" (all bought) to her apartment. "I also have one," Mösenbacher said, taking a gold-edged album from a shelf. She thumbed through the pages, pointing out pictures of her family. For weeks, Diamant had tolerated this vapid woman, who spoke viciously about the Jews, all to arrive at this point. He prayed that she had a photograph of Eichmann.

"You know, I had many admirers." Maria stopped at a photo of a man in his early thirties with a long, sharp nose and pursed lips. "This is Adolf . . . He was my boyfriend. Who knows what happened to him!? He probably didn't survive the war, otherwise he would surely have been in touch."

Diamant sat through two more hours of Maria's unpleasant company. The next morning the police seized the album on the pretense that they had received a tip that Mösenbacher was hiding stolen ration cards in it. Diamant could not keep his hands from trembling when he held the photograph.

Hundreds of copies were made and distributed to police and Allied investigators throughout Europe. Diamant himself delivered a copy to Simon Wiesenthal, who told him, "Now we know what he looks like. This is the first step in getting him."

Yet despite the photograph's wide distribution, there were no further clues to Eichmann's whereabouts.

Diamant was angry at the lack of progress. He continued to spend time with the Eichmann family in the hope of learning something new. A few months after his success with Maria Mösenbacher, he was out on the lake with Eichmann's three sons, who called him "Uncle Henry." Sitting in the boat, Diamant became overwhelmed by memories of the war: children taken from their mothers' arms, Jews fleeing through the streets, shootings and shootings and shootings.

When his mind cleared, he found himself gripping one of the oars and staring at Dieter Eichmann, who was laughing and

A youthful Vera
Eichmann, undated.

playing in the summer sunshine. Diamant had an urge to strike the child down in revenge — and the other two boys as well. Adolf Eichmann deserved to pay at least this price for what he had done, he silently raged. But then he relaxed his grasp on the oar and returned to shore.

Vera greeted him on his return, commenting that he looked strained.

"Nothing happened," Diamant said. "The children all behaved very well."

He swore never to go back to the house.

That December, Diamant left Austria, bound for Palestine. The United Nations resolution of November 27, 1947, had partitioned the territory for the establishment of a Jewish state. War was coming with the Arab states that opposed the creation of Israel, and Diamant knew where he wanted to be.

It was also clear to Simon Wiesenthal that the rest of the world was moving on. The start of the Cold War with the USSR drained the will and resources of the Allies away from pursuing Nazi war criminals. Justice took a backseat to preventing the spread of Communism. Wiesenthal hoped that the new state of Israel would support his continuing efforts.

Late in 1953, Wiesenthal arranged a meeting with an old

Austrian baron in Innsbruck to discuss stamps. A devoted monarchist who had suffered under Hitler, Baron Mast told his guest how upset he was that former Nazis were regaining high positions in the German government as if "nothing had changed." From his desk drawer, the baron passed Wiesenthal a letter from a German air force colonel who had never liked Hitler and who now lived in Argentina. "Beautiful stamps, aren't they?" the baron remarked. "But read what's inside."

Wiesenthal unfolded the letter and read its contents: "There are some people here we both used to know . . . Imagine who else I saw — and even had to talk to twice: that awful swine Eichmann who commanded the Jews. He lives near Buenos Aires and works for a water company."

"How do you like that?" the baron asked. "Some of the worst of the lot got away."

Astounded, Wiesenthal hurried back to his hotel to write down what he had read as well as the sender's name and address. Upon his return to Linz, he phoned the Israeli consul in Vienna and followed up by sending him a package that contained the contents of the baron's letter, a biography of Eichmann, examples of his handwriting, the photograph, and a chronicle of the eight-year search for him. Wiesenthal insisted that if the Israelis followed the trail, they would find Eichmann.

As the months passed without word from Israel, Wiesenthal became angry over the prospect that no action would be taken, but there was little he could do. He did not have the funds to go to Buenos Aires himself, nor did he speak Spanish. In addition, the Argentine government welcomed former Nazis and was largely hostile to Jews. Even if he found Eichmann, Wiesenthal knew that he would not be able to arrest him and get him out of the country. Still, he held out hope that the Israelis would take some action.

On March 30, 1954, that hope was lost as well. The Israeli consul met with Wiesenthal and told him that the Israelis did not have the resources to check out every rumor. They had enough to worry about in building the new nation and dealing with escalating tensions with Egypt. They needed to focus on the future, not on the past.

Soon after, Wiesenthal closed his office. He packed his papers and shipped the boxes, weighing almost twelve hundred pounds, to a museum in Israel. He kept a copy of the Eichmann file, but he was finished with chasing down this phantom about whom nobody else seemed to care. His disappointment at failing to find the war criminal kept him awake at night and haunted him through the day.

And so the hunt for Eichmann was abandoned and the trail went cold.

• • •

One December afternoon in 1956, Sylvia Hermann brought her new boyfriend, Nick, home to meet her parents. The family lived in Olivos, a mostly German suburb in the Vicente López district of Buenos Aires, Argentina. Sylvia had met Nick Eichmann at one of the local dance halls and had been out with him a few times. The introductions were made in German, and the young man sought out Sylvia's father's hand to shake it.

Over dinner, they spoke about Germany. Nick boasted how his father had been a high-ranking officer in the Wehrmacht, the German armed forces. The talk turned to the fate of the Jews. "It would have been better if the Germans had finished the job," Nick declared.

Lothar remained silent, though the statement stung. His dinner guest was unaware that Lothar was half-Jewish and had been imprisoned at the Dachau concentration camp for socialist activities in 1936. Fearful of the increasing Jewish persecution, he had emigrated with his Christian wife to Argentina soon after Kristallnacht, the night in November 1938 when Hitler's thugs had ransacked Jewish shops and homes. To avoid prejudice from the Argentine German community, Lothar had hidden his background. Sylvia had been raised a Christian, and few people, even close friends, knew of Lothar's Jewish lineage or that he had lost his sight as a result of Gestapo beatings.

Lothar quickly moved the conversation in another direction, avoiding an awkward scene. It was not as though the boy were alone in holding his opinion. During the war, the streets of Buenos Aires had been crowded with people raising Nazi banners and repeating Hitler's hateful philosophy. The defeat of Germany in World War II had not suddenly erased these sentiments.

Lothar Hermann in 1937, before he emigrated to Argentina.

Not long after, Sylvia ended her relationship with Nick. A few months later, the Hermanns moved from Olivos to Coronel Suárez, a village in the Pampas a few hundred miles southwest of Buenos Aires. Lothar started a new law practice, helping workers to apply for their retirement pensions. Sylvia had hopes of attending a university in the United States, but for the time being she was happy living with her parents.

One day, Sylvia was reading the newspaper *Argentinisches Tageblatt* to her father when she came across an article about a war-crimes trial in Frankfurt. One of the individuals listed as still being at large was the SS officer responsible for overseeing the mass murder of the Jews, Adolf Eichmann.

Sylvia stopped reading and looked up. Both she and Lothar immediately recalled the night when Nick Eichmann had talked openly about his father having served Germany well and how the Jewish people should have been exterminated. Sylvia put down the newspaper and told her father that Nick had never spoken much about his family, just that his mother had remarried after the war. She did not know if his father was alive. She had never been invited to Nick's home, nor did she even know where it was.

Lothar knew that many Nazis had escaped to Argentina after the collapse of the Third Reich, and he was certain that Nick's father was the war criminal Adolf Eichmann. He had to alert somebody, to do something. If he reached out to the German embassy in Buenos Aires, he was sure they would inform Eichmann, allowing him to escape again. Instead, he decided to write a letter to the German prosecutor mentioned in the newspaper article, Fritz Bauer, and to tell him that Adolf Eichmann was alive and well and living in Buenos Aires.

Fritz Bauer was the Attorney General of the state of Hesse and the bulldog of the West German court system. The son of a Jewish textile dealer, in 1933 he was sentenced to nine months in a concentration camp for his political activities. After his release, he fled to Denmark, but he returned after the war, convinced that it was his duty to help foster the new democracy.

Fritz Bauer in 1964.

Bauer replied to the Hermanns' letter and sent a few photographs of Adolf Eichmann, among which was the one Manus Diamant had found years before. Along with the photographs, Bauer included Eichmann's description and family details. The names and ages of Klaus and his brother Dieter matched those of the Eichmann boys Sylvia had met. She and Lothar were certain that they were Eichmann's sons. The question was whether their father was alive and sharing their house.

A few weeks later, Sylvia walked down Chacabuco Street in Buenos Aires. She and her father had taken the ten-hour train journey in from Coronel Suárez, then Sylvia had a long bus ride out to Nick Eichmann's neighborhood, where she hoped to find him and meet his father. She checked the numbers on each house until she reached 4261 Chacabuco.

The white bungalow at that address was typical of the area. It was no bigger than a few rooms and had a slanted terra-cotta roof. Sylvia went through the gate and knocked on the front door. As she waited for an answer, she spotted someone peeking through the curtains.

Several moments passed.

Sylvia stood at the door, knowing there was nobody to help her if things went wrong. She tried to appear as calm as possible while she waited.

Then a short, stout woman with a toddler in her arms opened the door. Sylvia introduced herself as a friend of Nick's. The woman said that she was his mother and cautiously welcomed the girl in the blue dress inside, asking if she wanted some coffee and cake.

"Yes," Sylvia said, and thanked her. Dieter was in the room, and she smiled at him. "Is Nick home?"

"No, he left an hour ago," Dieter replied.

As Sylvia sat down, a man wearing glasses came into the room. She guessed he was in his sixties, as Adolf Eichmann would have been. He walked with his head bent slightly forward, as if he was inspecting a scuff on the toe of his shoe.

"Good afternoon," Sylvia said.

He bowed slightly and said in perfect German, "Pleased to meet you, young lady."

"Are you Mr. Eichmann?" Sylvia asked bravely.

He did not answer.

"Are you Nick's father?"

The man hesitated before saying, "No . . . I'm his uncle." His biting tone matched the description that Sylvia had read in

Sylvia Hermann, undated.

Bauer's letter, but the photograph had been of a much younger man and was too blurry for her to be certain of his identity.

Nervous that she had pushed it too far, Sylvia steered the conversation to how she had recently graduated from high school and planned on studying foreign languages at a university. She asked the man if he spoke English or French, and he admitted knowing a few words of French from his time in Belgium during the war. The conversation soon trailed off, but he had relaxed a bit.

Before Nick's mother brought in the coffee, Nick himself came through the door. He was shocked to see Sylvia in his living room. "Who gave you my address? Who said you could visit me?"

Sylvia answered that a mutual friend had given her his address and that she had just wanted to see him while she was in Buenos Aires. "Did I do something wrong?" she asked.

The older man said there was no problem and that she was most welcome. Nick fell silent.

Wanting to leave as quickly as possible, Sylvia said that she had to go but that she hoped to return for a longer visit soon. There was an awkward moment of silence as the older man led Nick and Sylvia to the door.

"Thank you, Father," said Nick. "I'll see Sylvia to the bus."

While walking toward the bus station, Sylvia said that she was pleased to have met Nick's family. They walked some more, and then she asked the obvious question: Why had Nick addressed his uncle as "Father"?

Nick dismissed the question, explaining that it was merely a sign of respect. At the station, she said good-bye and watched him leave. The farther away he got, the safer she felt.

She hurried to meet her father and recounted everything that had happened at the house. They agreed to write to Bauer again with the story. It was plain to them that the man at the house was Nick Eichmann's father, not his uncle, and, given the other matching details, that he was without a doubt the Nazi, Adolf Eichmann.

סודי ביותר
לנמען בלבד

אל: פלט
מאת: גב

L.HERMANN
Gral.URQUIZA 85
Coronel Suarez F.C.N.G.R.
    ARGENTINA

Coronel Suarez, den 26.II.1958

Herrn Generalstaatsanwalt
Dr. Fritz Bauer
Feldbergstrasse 48
Frankfurt (Main)

Sehr geehrter Herr Doktor!

   Ich bestätige dankend den Erhalt Ihres Geschätzten v.21.1.58,
übersandt mit Luftpost und den Erhalt Ihres Briefes v.gleichen Datur
(Monopol-Metropole,Frankfurt Main) heute mir vorgezeigt und teile Ih
mit dass die Angelegenheit besprochen worden ist.

   Weitere Einzelheiten in der Sache, sowie ein ausführlicher Beri
wird Ihnen später, nach Abschluss der Verhandlungen zugehen.

   Ich wiederhole noch einmal dass Sie, sowie alle Teilnehmer an d
Sache mit strengste Diskretion zusichern müssen und werde ich persöe
mit allen Mitteln zu Verfügung stehen.

                         Mit freundlicher Hochachtung
                          ..Hermann

אזרח המדיבה – לסקטור הגרבחאי.

ב. אשתר עזבה את גרסביח בתאריך מאוחר יוהר, לפי ה מוקא
בשראם לאמריקאי מארה"ב שהכירה אותו ע"י הגרסביה, ומאז
צפלמו עקבוחיה. בעטר בסירובות ע"י הגרמים לבדוק
אצל משפחתה מקום מצאאת, אך ללא הועיל. לדעת המאור
ים מקום לחשוב שה"בעל השבד" של האטה איגלןאחר אלא
סימוס בעצצלר, שהחחתן אתה בשציה חחת שם חפש, ואולי לא
בחדין ארה"ב אלא כארגבטיבאי. אולם בבקודות אלח

Letters from Lothar Hermann to Fritz Bauer, 1957-8.

אחר שפיסוט עזב אותה ולקח לביתו גם את ילדדו של סימוס.
אולם זה כמרבן תיאורוחי, רש סיכוירים רבים יוחר
שאכן סלוסט הוא האדם,

CHAPTER 3

Near the crystal-blue waters of the Mediterranean, in the village of Sarona, Israel, stood an old stone house with a red tile roof. It looked like any other house in the Tel Aviv historic quarter, and none of the people who passed its door gave the place a second thought. Nor did they notice the spark plug of a man who came and went from it throughout the day.

At 5 feet 2, with jug ears and slate-blue eyes, he sometimes wore a neat, inexpensive suit, sometimes his shirt open to his thick chest. If anyone overheard him speaking — which would happen only if he *wanted* to be heard — they would hear short, sharp machine-gun bursts of Hebrew spoken with a slight Eastern European accent. He walked with a lively step and a straight back, looking like he always had a place to go. Israel was a young country populated by many people with a strong sense of purpose, and he was one of them.

The man was Isser Harel, Chief of the Institute for Intelligence and Special Operations, better known as the Mossad, Israel's secret intelligence agency. The old stone house was the organization's headquarters.

Harel was the youngest son of Orthodox Jews from Vitebsk, in central Russia. The family's prosperous business was seized after the 1917 Russian Revolution, and they moved to Latvia, where a young Isser survived his harsh new surroundings on the strength of his fists, a sphinxlike calm, and an omnivorous reading habit — everything from Russian classics to detective stories to Zionist literature. At sixteen, he decided to emigrate to Palestine. He obtained forged identity papers and traveled to Jaffa, the ancient port city at the southern end of Tel Aviv, with a small gun and a pocketful of bullets. When British officials searched the ship's passengers for weapons, Harel easily passed inspection, his revolver and ammunition hidden in a hollowed-out loaf of bread.

In 1942, fearing that Hitler might attack Palestine, Harel enlisted in the Haganah, a Jewish paramilitary organization. He was recruited to its intelligence service, the Shai. They ran a network of informants and spies, stole records, tapped phones, decoded messages, and built up weapons caches. Though not as educated or cultured as many Shai agents, Harel quickly took to the trade. He soon learned to read, interpret, and remember the most important details of an operational file, and he earned a reputation as a bloodhound, capable of tireless work digging up the smallest details. In 1947, he was promoted to run Shai operations in Tel Aviv, where he developed an extensive network of Arab informants.

On the eve of May 14, 1948, as David Ben-Gurion prepared to announce the creation of an independent Jewish state, Harel personally carried a message to him from an informant: "Abdullah is going to war — that's certain. The tanks are ready to go. The Arab Legion will attack tomorrow." Ben-Gurion sent several Israeli army units to establish a defense against the forces of King Abdullah I of Jordan, thwarting their surprise attack. Harel had earned the leader's attention.

Two months later, while Israel was still in the midst of war with Arab forces on all sides, Harel joined the other four section

Spymaster Isser Harel in 1965.

heads at Shai headquarters to reorganize Israeli intelligence and espionage operations. He was selected to run the Shin Bet, the internal security service (similar to the American FBI). The Arab forces withdrew in 1949, setting the legal boundaries of Israel where they are today. In 1952, Harel took over the Mossad.

Now, on a late September day in 1957, Harel had a rushed meeting at a nearby café with the Israeli Foreign Minister. The minister had urgent news from Germany that he did not want to share over the telephone: "Adolf Eichmann is alive, and his address in Argentina is known."

When he got back to his office, Harel tasked his secretary to retrieve whatever files they had on Eichmann. He had heard that the Nazi had played a leading role in the Holocaust and that there had been many rumors as to his whereabouts over the years. But that was all he knew.

The Mossad's lack of activity in pursuing war criminals reflected a lack of interest within Israeli society in general. Holocaust survivors, roughly a quarter of the population, rarely spoke of their experiences, both because it was too painful and because they did not want to focus on the past. They had a country to build.

Harel himself was haunted by what the Nazis had done to the Jewish people. The state of Israel existed in part to make sure that the Holocaust was never repeated. But he had never delved too deeply into the history of the genocide. His eighteen-hour working days were otherwise occupied.

Now he sat in silence with the Eichmann dossier his secretary had brought him. He read transcripts from the Nuremberg trials of high-ranking Nazis, SS files, testimony from Eichmann's staff members, and numerous reports of Eichmann's whereabouts.

Harel was completely unnerved by the portrait he formed. It was clear to him that Eichmann must be an expert in intelligence methods: He had managed to elude his pursuers for years. If they were going to bring this man to the justice he deserved, Harel knew one thing: They would need much more than an extradition request to the proper authorities in Argentina.

The first step was to see if the information that the Foreign Minister had given Harel in the café checked out. Harel wanted to know more about the minister's German contact, Fritz Bauer, and whether he was a reliable individual with whom to work. He decided to send one of his agents to Frankfurt to meet with him.

Pleased at the rapid Israeli response, Bauer explained that his source, whom he did not name, had given him facts about Eichmann that matched known details of his life, particularly regarding his family. The source had also provided an address where the family was living with a man of the same age as Eichmann. Bauer was willing to do whatever it took to get to Eichmann — even to risk his position as attorney general — and Harel concluded that his tip was solid.

In January 1958, he sent another operative, Yoel Goren, to the address Bauer had given him: 4261 Chacabuco Street in Olivos, Buenos Aires. Goren had spent several years in South America and spoke fluent Spanish. Harel warned him to be cautious, fearing that the slightest error might cause Eichmann to run again.

Over the course of a week, Goren went to Olivos several times. Chacabuco Street was an untrafficked, unpaved road, and strangers were eyed suspiciously. This made surveillance a challenge, but what Goren saw convinced him that there was little chance Adolf Eichmann lived there. The house was more suited to a single unskilled laborer than the family of a man who had once held a prominent position in the Third Reich. Adolf Eichmann was supposed to have extorted the fortunes of Europe's greatest Jewish families, not to mention the more limited wealth of many thousands of others. It seemed unlikely he could have been reduced to such poor quarters, even in hiding.

After taking several pictures of the house, Goren returned to Tel Aviv and reported to Harel that he had not seen anyone resembling Eichmann's description enter or leave while the house was under his surveillance. In his estimation, Adolf Eichmann could not possibly live in that "wretched little house" on Chacabuco Street.

Harel was now skeptical about Bauer's source and insisted on knowing his identity before getting more involved. Bauer agreed to write to Lothar Hermann to set up a meeting. When this was arranged, Harel sent the head of criminal investigations from the Tel Aviv police, Ephraim Hofstetter, to meet with Hermann.

Harel had tremendous faith in Hofstetter, a sober professional with twenty years of police experience. Polish by birth, Hofstetter had lost his parents and sister to the Holocaust. He spoke German fluently and could easily pretend to be working for Bauer — an important consideration, as Harel did not want the Eichmann investigation to be connected to Israel in any way. He told Hofstetter to find out how exactly Hermann knew about Eichmann, whether he was reliable, and whether he was holding anything back. He also asked him to identify the residents at 4261 Chacabuco.

Hofstetter arrived in Buenos Aires at the end of February, wearing winter clothes, only to discover that it was in fact the height of Argentina's summer. He was greeted outside the airport terminal by the laughter of a pale man with a bald pink head: Ephraim Ilani.

Ilani was a Mossad agent who had taken a leave of absence to study the history of Jewish settlements in Argentina. Fluent in Spanish (as well as nine other languages), Ilani knew the country well and had a wide network of friends and contacts in Buenos Aires thanks to his easy humor and gregarious nature. Harel had asked him to work closely with Hofstetter, who spoke only a few words of Spanish.

The two journeyed by overnight train to Coronel Suárez. The following morning, they stepped onto the platform of a dilapidated station. Apart from a single road bordered on either side by wooden houses, the remote town was little more than a stopping-off point before the endless grasslands of the Pampas.

It was hard to imagine a less obvious place for a clue to Adolf Eichmann's whereabouts.

After some inquiries, they got directions to Lothar Hermann's house. Hofstetter went to the door alone, Ilani staying behind in case there was any trouble. Several moments after Hofstetter knocked, the door opened. Hofstetter introduced himself to Hermann. "My name is Karl Huppert. I sent you a telegram from Buenos Aires to tell you I was coming."

Hermann indicated for Hofstetter to come into his living room. The Israeli policeman could not place what was wrong with Hermann or with the room, but something was amiss. Only when Hofstetter held out his letter of introduction and Hermann made no move to take it did he realize that the man was blind.

He couldn't believe it. Isser Harel had sent him to check on a sighting of Adolf Eichmann by a man who could not see.

He lost his skepticism, however, when Lothar Hermann and his wife, who came into the room to read the letter, explained in detail how they had first grown suspicious of Nick Eichmann and how their daughter had tracked down his address.

"Don't think I started this Eichmann business through any desire to serve Germany," Hermann said. "My only purpose is to even the score with the Nazi criminals who caused me and my family so much agony."

The front door opened, and Sylvia came in, calling out hello to her parents. She stopped on seeing Hofstetter, and her father introduced "Mr. Huppert." Sylvia confidently told him about her visit to the Eichmann house.

"Was there anything special about the way he spoke?" Hofstetter asked her.

"His voice was unpleasant and strident, just as Dr. Bauer described it in one of his letters."

Hofstetter asked her if these letters might have steered her wrongly to think the man at the house was Eichmann.

"No," she said bluntly. "I'm one hundred percent sure it was an unbiased impression."

"What you say is pretty convincing," Hofstetter said, impressed by her straightforwardness, not to mention her courage in going to the Eichmann house alone. Everything she said matched the information he had been given in Tel Aviv. "But it isn't conclusive identification. Vera Eichmann may have married again — we've heard many such rumors — and her children may have continued using their father's name." He explained that he needed to know the name of the person living with Vera and her sons, as well as where he worked. He also wanted to get any photographs of him or his family, any documents with his name, and, in the best case, a set of his fingerprints.

"I'm certain I'll be able to get you your proof," Hermann said. "I've got many friends in Olivos, as well as connections with the local authorities. It won't be difficult for me to get these things. However, it's obvious I'll have to travel to Buenos Aires again, my daughter too . . . This will involve further expense, and we simply can't afford it."

Hofstetter reassured Hermann that his people would cover any expenses. He instructed that all their correspondence be sent to him at an address in the Bronx, New York, care of an A. S. Richter. He tore an Argentine dollar in two and gave one half to Hermann. Anybody with the other half could be trusted.

After two hours of planning and discussion, Hofstetter thanked the family and left. He reported back to Harel that the

Hermanns were reliable but that more information was needed and that they seemed capable of gathering it.

On April 8, 1958, Sylvia and her father visited the land-records office in La Plata, the capital city of the province of Buenos Aires. A clerk brought them the public records on 4261 Chacabuco Street, and Sylvia read the details out to her father. An Austrian, Francisco Schmidt, had bought the small plot on August 14, 1947, to build two houses.

Eichmann was Austrian, Lothar knew. "Schmidt" must be the alias under which he was living. Excited by this discovery, Hermann and his daughter took a train to Buenos Aires to seek confirmation. Through a contact at the local electricity company, they found that two electric meters were registered at the address, under the names "Dagoto" and "Klement." When Hermann located the people who had sold Schmidt the land, he was given a description that resembled the one Bauer had sent and that his daughter had confirmed on her brief visit to the house.

The following month, the Hermanns returned to the city for five days to continue their investigation. They discovered a pho-tograph of Nick, but their attempts to get one of Eichmann, or his fingerprints or any identity documents, failed.

On May 19, Hermann wrote to "Karl Huppert" in New York, recounting their investigation of the past six weeks. "Francisco Schmidt is the man we want," he stated confidently. Further investigation would require more funds, he continued, and he should "hold all the strings" in pursuing the matter. Hermann was convinced that his discoveries would be met with a call to action. His letter wound its way from Argentina to New York to Israel, arriving at the Mossad headquarters in Sarona in June 1958.

Isser Harel was skeptical about its contents from start to finish. Just because Schmidt was listed as the owner of the land where a Nick Eichmann lived did not prove that Adolf Eichmann inhabited the house, nor under that alias. Hermann's demand for more funds and to "hold all the strings" stank of a potential scam. Hermann was too certain and wanted too much control — both factors Harel distrusted by instinct and experience. Harel trusted his intuition, and it told him that not only was Yoel Goren right in thinking that the former Nazi officer could not be living in the poverty he had witnessed, but also that the information Lothar Hermann had sent in his report was suspect at best and fantasy at worst.

Just to be sure, Harel cabled Ephraim Ilani in Buenos Aires to ask him to check on Francisco Schmidt. At the end of August, Ilani reported that Schmidt was not Eichmann, nor did he live at the Chacabuco Street address. He was merely the landlord. Hermann had the wrong man. Harel informed Bauer of his conclusions and ended all correspondence with Lothar Hermann.

The trail went cold once again.

CHAPTER 4

A year and a half later, in early December 1959, Fritz Bauer turned off the lights in his Frankfurt office and picked up his suitcase. He was headed to Israel, this time with certain proof that Adolf Eichmann was in Buenos Aires.

Bauer had set up a meeting with Haim Cohen, the Israeli Attorney General. Isser Harel had disappointed him by shelving the first investigation. He suspected that Harel would refuse to get involved unless he knew the identity of Bauer's new source. This was information Bauer could not reveal, because the person was too important politically. To this day, it is still a German state secret.

Bauer had no other option than to go to the Israelis. His suspicion that the West German government would not act against former Nazis had been proved again and again. He planned to ask Haim Cohen to put as much pressure as possible on Harel to investigate. As he headed out of the building and into a waiting car, Bauer could only hope that the fugitive was still within somebody's grasp.

●●●

Zvi Aharoni and Isser Harel sat in silence in the back of a chauffeur-driven sedan. The car threaded its way through the streets of the pine-covered Judean Hills outside Jerusalem.

Aharoni was the chief interrogator for the Shin Bet. Earlier in the day, Harel had informed him that they were expected at the Ministry of Justice in Jerusalem for a meeting with Haim Cohen and Fritz Bauer. Cohen had specifically asked for Aharoni, as they had worked together on several espionage and high-treason cases and were both gifted with the same cold, logical intelligence.

Zvi Aharoni.

It was only when Aharoni was in the car that Harel told him about Adolf Eichmann. Aharoni was not surprised. Harel's agents knew only what they needed to know — no more, no less. He *was* shocked that Harel had relied on the Hermanns to conduct the inquiries; he had been in Buenos Aires himself for six weeks earlier in the year on another mission and could have pursued some of the leads. However, one did not question the chief of the Mossad.

Aharoni scanned the reports sent from Lothar Hermann as the car made its way through the maze of steep streets to the Ministry of Justice on Jaffa Street. On arrival, Harel and Aharoni walked up to the second floor, where Cohen and Bauer were ready for them. Bauer launched straight into business, detailing the new intelligence he had received. The most important piece of information was the alias under which Eichmann lived: "Ricardo Klement." It was one of the names that had turned up in the Hermanns' investigation the previous year.

Bauer's bushy gray eyebrows flared as he spoke. He was incensed that the first investigation had dismissed the Hermanns' reports. "This is simply unbelievable!" he said angrily. "Here we have the name Klement: Two completely independent sources, who are strangers to each other, mention this name. Any second-class policeman would be able to follow such a lead! Just go and ask the nearest butcher or greengrocer and you will learn all there is to know about him!"

Harel tried to calm Bauer, explaining that this new intelligence changed the dynamic of the investigation. Bauer was still furious. He threatened to begin extradition proceedings through official German channels if the Israelis refused to act immediately. Though Harel thought that Bauer was bluffing, he reassured him that this would not be necessary. They wanted Eichmann found and were ready to act.

Cohen spoke up. "I want Zvi to go to Buenos Aires and check out this story once and for all. We can't play around with this any longer." Harel agreed, now persuaded that his interpretation of the Hermann reports had been wrong. Aharoni would go to Germany to collect the intelligence documents that Bauer had gathered over the past two years. Then he would travel to Argentina.

The meeting ended with warm handshakes.

● ● ●

On December 6, Israeli Prime Minister David Ben-Gurion ushered Isser Harel into his office. Though equal in height to his intelligence chief, the man known as the founding father of Israel had a much more commanding presence: the lantern jaw and instinctive aggressiveness of a fighter, combined with the wild white hair and searching intellect of an artist. In his early seventies, Ben-Gurion was nearing the end of his time as leader of the new nation, but his eyes were as bright and intelligent as the day in 1948 when he had announced the establishment of the state of Israel. Harel and Ben-Gurion were very close, having depended on each other over the past decade not only for Israel's benefit, but also for their own personal holds on its many levers of power.

Haim Cohen joined them shortly after, and Harel recounted their conversation with Fritz Bauer, emphasizing that the German Attorney General now had intelligence detailing where Eichmann lived and under what alias. Ben-Gurion was impressed by the courage Bauer had shown in coming to them again — this time personally — with the information. Harel told the Prime Minister that Bauer had threatened extradition proceedings in West Germany if Israel failed to pursue his leads.

"Prevent Bauer from taking this step," Ben-Gurion said. "If Eichmann is there, we will capture him in order to bring him here."

Harel knew this type of operation would present enormous challenges and tax the Mossad's limited resources. A quicker, easier solution might be to assassinate Eichmann. His people were well practiced in these operations: One day the Argentine police would discover Ricardo Klement in a car crash or some other mishap, and the world would not need to know that Adolf Eichmann was dead — nor that the Israelis had killed him.

But Ben-Gurion was clear. He wanted Eichmann alive to stand trial in Israel for his crimes against the Jewish people.

Cohen had concerns about this plan. Legally, West Germany had much more of a right to try Eichmann than Israel, a state that had not existed when the crimes were committed. Ben-Gurion instructed the Israeli Attorney General to come up with a justification. As for the capture operation, he had complete faith in Harel, writing in his diary that night, "Isser will deal with it."

• • •

Three weeks later, on Christmas Eve, those in West Germany who looked fondly on their Nazi past made their presence known. In Cologne, two young men painted huge swastikas and "*Juden Raus*" ("Jews Out") across the walls of a synagogue and on a memorial to those who had resisted Hitler. In the following days, anti-Semitic attacks and demonstrations broke out across West Germany, and police were stationed outside synagogues and Jewish cemeteries to prevent further desecrations. In total, 685 Jewish locations throughout the country were vandalized. These were more than the isolated actions of a few hooligans, and Jewish leaders in West Germany made it clear that the scene "evoked pictures that bring to mind the November days of 1938," referring to Kristallnacht.

West German Chancellor Konrad Adenauer promptly broadcast on the radio that these acts were intolerable, but it was plain that much more was needed to stop the rise of neo-Nazism. The German Reich Party, a radical group with Nazi sympathies, had made gains in a recent election. Membership in militant and nationalistic organizations was increasing, as were the numbers of newsletters and daily papers, book clubs, and discussion groups whose followers despised the "Bonn democracy" (referring to the capital of West Germany) and wanted to "correct the accepted facts" about Hitler and German war guilt.

A *New York Times* reporter described an "almost nation-wide need to pull the blinds on the past" in West Germany. Schoolteachers were found to be teaching incorrect information about Hitler's regime. A ninth-grade textbook devoted only a single paragraph to the "Jewish question" during World War II. Extermination camps went without mention.

All of these trends were noticed in Israel with grave concern. Soon after the Cologne incident, the Foreign Affairs and Defense Committee of the Knesset, Israel's parliament, asked Isser Harel about the possibility of a Nazi revival. Even to these high officials, Harel could not reveal the major blow he intended to deliver to such a revival: the capture of Adolf Eichmann. Harel was now convinced that Ben-Gurion was right. Bringing the fugitive to justice and airing his crimes in a public trial would remind the world of the Nazi atrocities, and the need to remain vigilant against any groups that aimed to repeat them.

People gather outside the desecrated synagogue in Cologne, Germany, 1959.

CHAPTER 5

On March 1, 1960, Zvi Aharoni stepped up to Immigration Control at Buenos Aires's Ezeiza Airport. His Israeli diplomatic papers identified him as Mr. Rodan of the Foreign Ministry. He explained in his rough Spanish that he had traveled to Argentina to investigate reports of an outbreak of anti-Semitism in South America. The guard studied the passport and then the man who had handed it to him. Aharoni had the kind of long, sober face that made it difficult to guess his thoughts, which was always an advantage in his interrogation work.

The guard stamped his documents without inspecting the sealed diplomatic pouch Aharoni carried under his arm, which contained everything the Israelis knew about Eichmann. Aharoni knew that another "maybe" in the Eichmann file would be useless. Harel needed a definitive answer before he could launch a mission.

Aharoni was met at the airport and brought to the Israeli Embassy by a man known only as "Yossef," the embassy head of security and the only person in Argentina aware of the reason for his visit. Aharoni locked his Eichmann files in an embassy safe; after long study, he knew most of the facts by heart.

Two days later, he rolled slowly down Chacabuco Street in a rented Fiat. "Roberto," a twenty-year-old Argentine student with a thick black mustache, sat next to him, studying a street map. Roberto was one of the *sayanim* — Jewish volunteers who were available to help Mossad agents with surveillance, transport, safe houses, or medical aid, or simply by standing on a corner and waiting for a messenger. They went by aliases, so even now their real names are not known. Without them, the small Israeli secret service would not have had anything like the reach it did. Having volunteered for other Mossad operations in the past, Roberto knew to keep his inquiries to a minimum.

Driving past 4261 Chacabuco, Aharoni stole a glance at the small house with its unkempt garden. He stopped a few blocks away on a side street, wondering how he could get a good look at whoever lived there. He fished a postcard of a tropical island, which he had bought at the airport, out of his pocket. He told Roberto to write on the back in Spanish, "Have just returned. Best regards, George," along with a fictitious name and address. He also instructed him to put "Dagosto" (a variation of Dagoto, the name under which one of the electric meters at 4261 Chacabuco was registered) and 4263 Chacabuco in the sender box. The address was nonexistent, but the card would give Roberto a reason to ask neighbors if they knew the sender. Because the postcard lacked a stamp and postmark, Aharoni warned Roberto not to let anyone inspect it too closely.

Roberto walked off while Aharoni stayed in the car. Three years had passed since Sylvia Hermann had walked down this street. The Nazi fugitive might well have moved house, and if he had, the chance of finding him again would be slim in a city of more than five million people spread across seventy-one square miles.

Twenty minutes later, Roberto hurried back to the car. He waved the postcard and slid into the passenger's seat. He explained that he had spoken to a young girl about the Dagosto family and had peered, undetected, through the windows of

4261 Chacabuco. Nobody in the neighborhood was named Dagosto, but Roberto had seen some painters working inside the house. The house was unoccupied. The Eichmanns had moved.

Aharoni was undeterred. The next day, March 4, "Juan," a baby-faced eighteen-year-old Argentine with a constant grin, opened the gate at 4261 Chacabuco Street. He had in his hand a gift-wrapped box containing an expensive cigarette lighter. It was addressed to Nikolas Klement, Vicente López, 4261 Chacabuco. Slipped under the ribbon was a note in flowery script written by an embassy secretary: "For my friend Nicki, in friendship, on his birthday."

Aharoni had given Juan instructions to go to the address and find out where "Nick Klement" had moved. His cover was that he had a gift to deliver. Under no circumstances, Aharoni warned, was Juan to go to the new address himself.

Not finding a bell at the gate, Juan called out for Nick Klement. When nobody answered, he stepped around to the back of the house, where he found a man and a woman. "Excuse me, please," Juan said. "But do you know whether Mr. Klement lives here?"

"You mean the German?" the man asked.

"I don't know."

"The one with the three grown sons and the little boy?"

"I don't know," Juan said. Truly, he had no idea.

"Those people used to live here, but now they have moved. Maybe two to three weeks ago." The man suggested that Juan speak to one of the workmen inside the house.

Juan showed the card and gift to a carpenter. "Can you tell me where I can find him?" Juan asked. "I have to deliver it personally."

The carpenter told him that the family had moved to a neighborhood called San Fernando. He offered to take Juan to where one of Klement's sons worked as a mechanic, just a block away.

Approaching the garage on the next corner, the carpenter pointed out a moped he said belonged to Klement's son. Then he shouted, "Dito!" A young man in his late teens, wearing oil-stained overalls, headed over. "This guy would like to speak to your father," the carpenter told him.

Juan had no idea if he was looking for the father or the son, only that the addressee's name was Nick Klement. He explained why he had gone to the house and that he had just learned the Klements had moved. Curtly, Dito said he had his facts straight.

"Where have you moved to?" Juan asked.

"To Don Torcuato."

Juan hesitated a moment before asking Dito to give the package to Nick Klement.

"I'd like to know who gave you that," Dito said.

In keeping with the cover story Aharoni had provided, Juan explained that he did not know the name or anything else about the young lady who had given his friend, a bellboy at an upmarket hotel, the package to deliver. He asked could he just have Mr. Klement's address in order to make the delivery himself.

Dito shook his head, saying that the area had no street addresses. At last, however, he agreed to take the package. Sensing that he had pressed him enough, Juan left.

Listening to Juan's report, Aharoni grew excited and thanked him for a job well done. Now he knew for certain that a German family named Klement had lived at the Chacabuco address until only a few weeks before. They had four sons, one of whom was roughly the same age and had a similar-sounding name to Dieter Eichmann. Not only was the trail still alive, they might even have found one of Eichmann's boys.

On a map, Aharoni located the two neighborhoods to where Juan had been told the family had moved. Don Torcuato and San Fernando were more than three miles apart. Given this discrepancy, as well as the facts that the family had not left a forwarding address and Dito had refused to give his, Aharoni concluded that the Klements had something to hide — another sign that they might be the Eichmanns.

Aharoni decided to risk finding out more information from the workers at the house. Later that day, he drove "Lorenzo" to 4261 Chacabuco. The *sayan* had the looks, suit, and smooth manner of the salesman he was pretending to be. Two visits on the same day was incautious, and this second one only confirmed that Ricardo Klement had once lived at the house.

Confident in what he had learned, Aharoni cabled Harel a message in a prearranged code: "The driver is red," meaning that Klement was likely Eichmann. He added that their target had recently moved and that he was attempting to locate him. Once Aharoni sent the code "The driver is black," Harel would know that Eichmann had been found and the operation to capture him could be set in motion.

On March 8, Aharoni and Juan waited in the Fiat on Monteagudo Street, keeping watch on the early-evening traffic. Anybody leaving Dito's shop would have to drive by them to reach the neighborhoods of San Fernando or Don Torcuato to the north. Aharoni was depending on Dito to lead him to Eichmann, and this was the third afternoon they had spent waiting for him to pass.

At 5:15 P.M., a dirt-spattered black moped whirred past the Fiat from the direction of the shop. Its driver, a man in his fifties, wore dark glasses. Riding behind him, holding his shoulders, was a young blond man wearing overalls. Juan pointed him out, almost certain it was Dito.

Aharoni started the car and shifted quickly into gear. He followed the moped through the traffic, remaining unseen. Ten minutes later, after a series of turns, the moped swung down an alley by a railroad station in San Isidro, the neighborhood directly southeast of San Fernando.

The young man dashed into a building, coming out two minutes later. Again, Aharoni and Juan followed. When they reached the center of San Fernando, they lost the bike among the cars and trucks jammed around the main square. Catching sight of it again, Aharoni turned off the square to follow and found himself abruptly halted by a funeral procession. He slammed his hand on the steering wheel as the moped disappeared from view.

Over the next week, Aharoni attempted to trail Dito with two other teams of sayanim. On the first night, during a heavy downpour, the moped didn't show. On the second, this time in a rented station wagon, Aharoni followed the moped, again with two riders, back to San Fernando. There he switched cars with two of the young Argentines helping him. He almost lost the moped again around the square. When the bike reached Route 202, the major highway that ran past Don Torcuato, Aharoni trailed at a distance, since only a few cars remained on the road. The moped pulled up at a roadside kiosk close to a railway embankment. A scattering of houses and wooden huts marked the barren, flat land. Aharoni slowed down as he drove past, then he circled back toward San Fernando.

On the third night, Aharoni and Juan shadowed a lone young man who left the garage on a moped. When he stopped at a house on the way to San Fernando, Aharoni sent Juan out for a closer look. A few minutes later, he came back and said the young man was probably not Dito.

Aharoni swelled with anger. They had wasted a week since Juan first went into the house on Chacabuco, learning nothing. Now they had followed the same individual several nights in a row, at great risk of being spotted, and they were still unsure if they were trailing the right person. This had to stop. They had to get either the new address of the Klement family or confirmation that it was indeed Dito they were tailing.

"Go back tomorrow," Aharoni instructed Juan. "Tell him your friend is angry. He claims that you never delivered the present and he wants the money from you. Get the address where they live so you can speak to Mr. Klement, or at least make sure you have a good look at the boy. Don't tell me you're not sure: I need a yes or a no."

On March 12, as instructed, Juan returned to 4261 Chacabuco Street. The carpenter who he had met before was there, and he felt bad for Juan. Although he didn't know the street name of the Klements' new house, he could give exact directions to get there: Juan should go to the San Fernando station, take the 203 bus to Avellaneda Street, and ask at the corner kiosk for the Germans' house. It was an unfinished brick house with a flat roof only a few hundred yards from there.

Juan thanked the carpenter and walked over to the mechanic's shop. Dito came out into the yard. "And what do you want this time?" he said. Juan told his story again, how his friend was facing a charge of 500 pesos.

Dito grew hostile. "How come? If that girl wanted to send it to my brother, why didn't she write down his real name?"

Later that afternoon, Aharoni waited nervously for Juan at a café near the Israeli Embassy. When the young man finally appeared, his usual smile was gone, and he looked exhausted. "What happened?" Aharoni asked, now more worried than before.

Juan explained halfheartedly that he had good directions to the Klements' new house. Aharoni was flummoxed as to why this would depress him: This was what they had been trying to find out. Juan then said, "We followed the wrong guy. The name's not Klement. It's Eichmann."

Aharoni almost leapt from his seat onto the table, but he kept himself calm. "Ah. Never mind. Don't worry about it," he said. He thanked Juan for a job well done and urged him not to speak to anybody, ever, about their time together. In parting, Aharoni promised, "We'll find the right guy."

The next day, Aharoni crawled along Route 202 in his rented station wagon and passed a kiosk on his left. The directions the carpenter had given Juan had played out perfectly so far. Aharoni remembered coming to this same kiosk a few days before while following the moped. A railway embankment crossed the road, but otherwise the area was level and almost completely feature-less. It was a poor, sparsely populated section of San Fernando, without telephone or electrical lines.

He spotted a one-story brick house with a large wooden door and tiny windows. The masonry was unfinished and the roof flat — just as the carpenter had described. With its barred windows and surrounding chicken-wire fence, the house looked more like a jail than a home. Aharoni noticed a woman sitting on the edge of the porch. A young boy, no older than six, played at her feet. Aharoni suspected he was looking at Vera Eichmann and her fourth son, who would have been born since she came to Argentina. He continued under the railway bridge, stunned at the poverty in which the family was living — worse even than the Olivos house. But it was the right place; Aharoni was sure of that. Now all he needed was proof that Klement was indeed Eichmann.

On March 16, 1960, Zvi Aharoni went into the San Fernando civil administration headquarters with "Michael," an architect who had emigrated from Israel several years before. They knew that no one could buy land and build a house without leaving a paper trail. Using false names and a cover story — that they worked for an American company that wanted to build a sewing factory — they asked for the names of the people living near where the rail line intersected Route 202. The clerk guaranteed an answer the next day.

Aharoni wanted to photograph the woman he had seen sitting on the porch with her son, to compare her with pictures he had of Vera Eichmann. He drove with Michael to the Klement home, and they parked in front of a neighbor's house. Michael carried a clipboard, and Aharoni had a briefcase with a hidden camera. The lens was behind a hole in the side, and a small button by the handle took the photographs.

The neighbor, a middle-aged woman, came out of her house when she saw them. While they were speaking with her, Aharoni snapped a few pictures of the area. Then a black-haired woman in her early twenties approached from the direction of the Klement house. By her looks and accent, she was a native Argentine, and her tone and body language made it clear she wanted them gone.

"What's the name of your employer?" she demanded. "What sort of factory were you planning?"

She clearly didn't believe their cover. Aharoni wanted to get out of there straightaway. They were in serious danger of being exposed. As Michael began to explain their sewing business, the woman cut him off, wondering aloud why anyone would want to build in an area without electricity or water. Surely they were up to no good.

"It's possible there's been a mistake and we've confused the area," Aharoni said before turning to Michael and pointing toward the railway. "Let's continue our inquiries on the other side."

They thanked the woman for her help, retreated to the car, and drove away. Aharoni prayed he had not just tipped off Adolf Eichmann. He needed to be more careful.

The next day he learned that their efforts to get a list of land-owners had failed. The building office did not keep records on the area, though Aharoni did learn that the street the house was on was named Garibaldi Street.

Michael had an idea. Much of that part of San Fernando had been purchased by a single company that had then resold the land in smaller lots. That company might have the information they needed. The next day, he presented Aharoni with a piece of paper. "I found the registered owner of plot 14," Michael said. "It's Veronika Liebl de Fichmann."

"I don't know how to thank you. That's exactly what I've been looking for," Aharoni said. The misspelled name had to be either a clerical error or a deliberate attempt to confuse searchers. Now Aharoni just needed to see Ricardo Klement for himself.

The next day, he went to San Fernando. He had switched cars yet again and was now behind the wheel of a black DeSoto. With

Surveillance photos of Eichmann's house on Garibaldi Street.

him was an embassy secretary, and together they looked like any couple out for a weekend drive.

Coming down Route 202, Aharoni looked over at the Klement house on Garibaldi Street. A man was in the yard, taking down the washing. Aharoni slowed down. He was at least fifty years old, had a thin build, and was probably between 5 feet 7 and 5 feet 9 inches tall, balding, with a high, sloped forehead.

Before Aharoni could reach for his briefcase camera, the man collected the last garment from the line and returned to the house. But Aharoni knew the face, no question. He had spent hours staring at photographs of it in the Eichmann file.

"Why are you looking so happy?" the embassy secretary asked. He had not realized that a wide grin had spread across his face.

"I just remembered that today is my mother's birthday," he said. "Let's go and celebrate."

Later, he sent Harel a cable with a single line of code: "The driver is black."

Photo of Eichmann that Aharoni likely used to identify him in Argentina.

CHAPTER 6

In Tel Aviv, Isser Harel was ready for Aharoni's message.

Over the past few weeks, with classical music playing on his transistor radio, he had run through the many challenges they would face if the operation went ahead. It would occur almost 9,000 miles away, in a country few of his agents knew and whose language even fewer of them spoke. They would be traveling under false identities, completely alone and without official cover. Their target had been an officer in the SS, one of the most deadly security forces ever known. He had intimate knowledge of surveillance and operational tactics, and he knew how to defend himself. During the war, he had never moved about unarmed.

Buenos Aires had a large German community, including some former Nazis. There were many people within the Argentine halls of power who had no love for Israel or the Jews. At such a distance, communication between Harel's agents and Tel Aviv would not be easy or quick. If the agents were discovered, they would face imprisonment or worse. Israel would have no end of international political problems, and the black mark against the Mossad would inhibit its activities in other countries.

For all these reasons, the mission could not be allowed to fail.

It would comprise three parts: First, they needed to capture Eichmann alive, without being seen. Second, they would have to keep him in a secure location, avoiding detection, for an indeterminate period of time, until, third, they could smuggle him out of Argentina. Nobody could know who had taken him, or how, until he was in an Israeli prison and all Harel's agents were safe.

If the mission succeeded, Harel knew that not only would the Mossad earn its place among the top intelligence agencies in the world, but also — much more important — the Jewish people would see justice done to one of the leading organizers of the Holocaust. The world would be forced to remember what had happened, and it would be reminded that such horrors must never be repeated.

• • •

Zvi Aharoni lay on an old mattress in the back of a Ford pickup, peering out with his binoculars through a hole cut in the tarpaulin that covered it. His driver for the day, yet another sayan, was inside the nearby kiosk eating a late breakfast. They had parked facing the kiosk, which gave Aharoni a perfect view of the Eichmann house, 160 yards away.

Although Aharoni was certain that he had identified their target, he had set himself one more task. He wanted a good photograph of Eichmann. While watching for him to come out of his house, he took several shots of the surrounding area for the operations team that would execute the capture. He also sketched a map of the neighborhood, with key roads and landmarks.

At noon, Eichmann unexpectedly strode past the truck from the direction of the kiosk. He must have left the house that morning before Aharoni had arrived. Eichmann headed down Route 202, then turned left before Garibaldi Street, crossing an

The truck used by Aharoni during surveillance.

empty field to get to his house. Aharoni got a long, clear look at him. He was dressed in brown slacks, an overcoat, and a green tie. He wore glasses, was mostly bald, and had a prominent nose and broad forehead. He walked slowly, with a deliberate gait.

Aharoni felt even more sure that this was the right man. Unfortunately, however, Eichmann was too far away for him to get a good photograph. For the next hour, Aharoni watched. When Eichmann got to his house, he spoke to a boy playing in the garden, straightening the child's shirt and trousers. He swatted at a cloud of flies around the front door before going inside. Later, he came out wearing casual cotton pants, bought some bread from a horse-drawn cart, and fetched something from the shed. His son Dieter came home, and the whole family went into the house, probably to have lunch.

Later that night, Aharoni was back in San Fernando for more surveillance. He drove a faded red jeep and was accompanied by "Avi," an embassy official, and his wife. Aharoni had seen couples parked in the area at night and knew that the two would provide good cover. Wearing overalls and carrying a pair of binoculars, he left the jeep and crept toward the house. His aim was to get a look at the interior, in case the operations team needed to go inside.

The dark night was ideal for such a goal. However, there were no lights on in the house. Aharoni returned to the jeep only a few minutes after he had left it. To his shock, it was gone. He walked around the area, and before long he saw the jeep, fifteen yards away, lying in the ditch beside the road. He could hardly believe his eyes.

Avi and his wife were huddled in the ditch beside the vehicle. They had tried to turn it around without switching on the headlights, thinking they might need to make a fast getaway. Avi had not noticed that the road was raised, and he had backed straight into the ditch. Aharoni was livid, but his anger paled beside his fear that the Eichmann family, whose house was less than 150 yards away, might discover them. Either they or their neighbors would realize that the strangers were all foreign — and possibly that they were Israelis — and Eichmann would know without doubt that he was under surveillance. They would never see him again.

"Let's go," Aharoni said, thinking fast. If they left the jeep in the ditch, it would look very suspicious. Eichmann might even be able to trace Aharoni's alias through the rental agency. But they could not be seen under any circumstances.

They ran down Avellaneda Street. Luckily, a bus appeared a few minutes later. When they reached the San Fernando bus station, Aharoni called the only person he could think of who could get the jeep out of the ditch quietly and quickly: Yitzhak Vardi. Vardi was an Israeli financier who had once worked in intelligence for the Israeli Foreign Ministry but who now led the United Jewish Appeal in South America, based in Buenos Aires.

Vardi understood the critical nature of the situation. Less than an hour later, he drove up to the bus station in his huge Chevrolet, with a tow truck following behind. By the time they reached the vehicle, someone had stolen one of the tires. While Aharoni put the spare tire on the jeep, some of the neighbors came out to see what all the lights and commotion were about. The Argentine tow-truck driver assured them that nobody had been hurt, it was just a minor accident. The Israelis kept their mouths shut.

Aharoni did not see Dieter or his father in the crowd and breathed a little more easily. Within a few minutes, the jeep was back on the road. Aharoni thanked Vardi and drove away.

On Sunday, April 3, Aharoni risked one last return to San Fernando. "Rendi" was with him — a sayan who looked old enough to be out searching for a house for his family, which was his cover story. Aharoni had taught him how to hold the briefcase camera and take pictures.

After they parked, Rendi cut across the field to the house. Through his binoculars, Aharoni watched anxiously as he strode up to Eichmann and Dieter, who were working in their yard. Aharoni knew he was asking how much it would cost to build a house in the area. Two minutes passed. Then three.

Rendi's photograph of Eichmann outside his house on Garibaldi Street.

Then four. Rendi chatted with the two men as if they were old friends.

At last he walked away, in the direction of Eichmann's neighbors' house, as instructed by Aharoni, to talk to them as well. Then he headed back to the kiosk, where he waited for a bus to San Fernando. He told Aharoni later that he was confident he had not been suspected of taking photographs.

Three days later, when Aharoni received the developed film, he was delighted to see that Rendi had taken perfectly focused shots of Adolf Eichmann and his son at three or four different angles, all of them up close. Aharoni had his picture, and was satisfied that he had completed his mission.

Isser Harel had ordered Aharoni to return to Israel as soon as possible to provide a full report. He flew to Paris on April 8. The next day, he boarded the flight to Tel Aviv and was shocked to see Harel himself coming down the aisle. Harel sat down next to him, behaving as if he were a total stranger. Only after the plane took off did he turn to Aharoni to ask, "Are you definitively sure this is our man?"

Aharoni pulled a negative from his coat pocket. "I have not the slightest doubt. Here's the picture."

Harel studied the photograph for a moment, then said, "Okay. In that case, we're going to get him."

CHAPTER 7

How had the powerful Adolf Eichmann, a major figure in one of the most frightening empires the world has ever known, come to live in a shack in Argentina?

In February 1945, Argentina's Vice President and Secretary of War, Juan Perón, brought together the leading lights of the country's influential German community, most of them fervent supporters of the Third Reich. Perón, a Machiavellian opportunist, announced to the group that since it looked likely that the Axis would lose to the Allies, Argentina was ending its neutrality and declaring war on Germany.

"It's a mere formality," he explained, done to save the country from punishment from the Allies when the fighting ended. He promised not to abandon his German friends. He wanted Nazi scientists and engineers to come to Argentina to benefit its military research and industrialization. He also felt it was his duty to help anyone who immigrated from Germany to build a new life — no matter what he or she had done during the war.

The Argentine secret service then established an escape network with bases throughout Europe. The network's agents financed operations, bribed local officials, and orchestrated safe houses and transportation. Between the immigration office in Argentina and the various Argentine consulates in Europe, they produced all the necessary paperwork for Nazis to flee the continent.

Argentina was not alone in providing sanctuary for former Nazis. Postwar Europe was full of people on the run. Fake passports, forged identification papers, and willing smugglers were all easy to find. The Allies also smuggled out a number of war criminals, among them former SS officers, who were then recruited for intelligence activities against the Soviet Union and its satellites. In fact, the United States used some of the same routes and safe houses to smuggle people out of Europe as Argentina did.

Adolf Eichmann had spent time in prisoner-of-war camps at the end of the war, but he escaped and disappeared before the authorities realized his true identity. He went into hiding for three years in the forests of Germany, working as a lumberjack and then a chicken farmer. In 1948, he decided it was safe to make an attempt to leave the country. The British had ended their efforts to try war criminals, and the Americans were now preoccupied with the Russians.

He contacted "Günther," an underground agent on the Argentine network, through coded newspaper advertisements, and paid three hundred marks, one-fifth of his savings, for his help. Günther gave him his instructions, and Eichmann traveled by train to Munich, nervous that he might be exposed at any moment.

Munich was swarming with border police on the lookout for fugitives. Eichmann trembled as he filled out a hotel registration form, signing it "Otto Heninger." After a week of anxious waiting, a local hunter made contact with him and guided him across the border into Austria.

There he had two contacts. The first, a former SS lieutenant, sent him packing, huffing, "They really send every damn tramp this way." The second brought him to an inn near the Brenner Pass in the Alps between Austria and Italy. French soldiers were active in the area, so Eichmann had to be hidden in the inn's attic. Several days later, the innkeeper judged it was safe to leave and took him along the edge of the pass. Eichmann was not allowed to bring his suitcase; the innkeeper was afraid it would arouse suspicions if they came across a patrol. A mile over the border into Italy, a priest in black robes on a bicycle met the two men on the road. The priest had Eichmann's suitcase with him.

The innkeeper returned to Austria, and the priest arranged for a car to take Eichmann and himself to Merano, a Tyrolean village in northern Italy. Eichmann spent the night at a castle, a safe house for fleeing Nazis. The next day, he received a new identity card, issued by the town hall of a neighboring village, Termeno. His new name would be Ricardo Klement. The underground agent who brought the ID also had a landing permit for his final destination: Buenos Aires.

On May 31, 1950, Eichmann left Merano for the city of Genoa, arriving at nightfall. The following day, he presented himself at the local headquarters of the International Committee of the Red Cross. He handed the official his landing permit and ID, along with a letter of reference that stated that Ricardo Klement was a refugee from the war and could not obtain a travel document from any other source. The official approved Eichmann's application for a Red Cross passport without question. He took his fingerprints and photograph, attached one copy to the cardboard passport, and marked it with a Red Cross stamp dated June 1, 1950. An elated Eichmann walked out of the office feeling like a real person again.

On July 17, Eichmann made his way down to the port of Genoa. Carrying his suitcase and wearing a new suit, a bow tie, and a black hat, for all the world he looked like a traveling salesman. He boarded the passenger ship *Giovanna C* and deposited his bag in his third-class berth. Then he went to the upper deck to watch the departure. As the ship steamed out of the harbor, Eichmann felt a rush not only of relief but also of triumph. The chance of discovery by the Allies would be next to nothing in Argentina, especially if he was careful.

Eichmann had 485 pesos in his pocket when he arrived in Buenos Aires, the equivalent of $35 ($850 in today's money). With limited funds and no work papers, he might have fallen on hard times if not for the assistance of the German Argentine network. Carlos Fuldner, the operator of the Argentine ratline,

Eichmann's Red Cross passport.

shepherded Eichmann into his new life, finding him an apartment and introducing him to other escapees. He secured Eichmann a job in a metal shop and facilitated the approval of his Argentine ID card by the Buenos Aires police. By October 1950, with these papers in hand, Eichmann was now wholly and completely Ricardo Klement, a permanent resident of Argentina and legally able to work.

Two years later, when Eichmann requested that his wife and three sons join him, the network helped him again, secretly contacting Vera on his behalf. Eichmann first wrote to her at Christmas 1950, saying that "the uncle of your children, whom everybody presumed dead, is alive and well — Ricardo Klement." Later he sent her money and instructions for travel.

When Vera and the boys arrived in Buenos Aires on July 28, 1952, Eichmann had them met at the port and brought to a nondescript hotel — a precaution in case they had been followed. When he appeared in the doorway, his wife cried with joy. Despite her delight, she couldn't help but notice that her husband had aged dramatically. His stoop was more pronounced, his face looked drawn and gray, and his hair had thinned.

"I am your Uncle Ricardo," Eichmann said to his sons. Klaus was now sixteen, Horst twelve, and Dieter ten. Thinking that their father had been dead for years, the two younger sons did not question him. But Klaus knew that this man was his father. Eichmann gave them one hundred pesos each, and the boys ran off to explore. The two youngest bought ice cream and candy, and Klaus, taking after his father, bought his first pack of cigarettes.

Once Eichmann and Vera were alone, she brought out the pile of newspaper clippings she had collected about the terrible crimes he had committed. She wanted an explanation. Eichmann

Eichmann in Argentina.

became enraged. "Veronika," he said, "I have not done a single Jew to death, nor given a single order to kill a Jew."

She never asked him about the past again.

• • •

Eight years after the Eichmann family settled in Argentina, Adolf Eichmann's past caught up with him.

Back in Tel Aviv, Isser Harel briefed Rafi Eitan, the Shin Bet Chief of Operations, on recent developments in the search for Eichmann and on Aharoni's work of the previous three weeks. "I'm putting you in as the commander," Harel informed him. "A. Take the most suitable men for the job, since you know what it will take to do it. B. Volunteers only. Ask each man if he is ready to volunteer. I don't know how this will end, and if they are caught, theoretically they could even end up with a life sentence in an Argentine jail."

There was never a more unlikely looking individual for the role of mission leader than Rafi Eitan, who was extremely short-sighted and wore Coke-bottle glasses that made his eyes seem to bulge out from his face. He was only slightly taller than Harel, with the barrel chest and muscular arms of a farmer. But he spoke with confidence about his ability to find and lead the right men for the job. "None of them will hesitate," Eitan said quietly.

On April 10, Avraham Shalom was summoned to meet with Harel. Thirty-three years old, Shalom had the stout body of a wrestler and the kind of common, indistinctive face people usually forgot once he left the room. He was originally from Vienna, and when he was nine, he had been beaten so badly by thirty of his Austrian classmates — some of whom he thought were his closest friends — that he had to stay in bed for two weeks to recover.

They had beaten him because he was Jewish. His teachers had watched.

Now he was the Deputy of Shin Bet Operations, and he had just returned to Israel from an intense undercover mission when Harel called. Shalom went directly to Mossad headquarters in Sarona, where Harel sat him down and asked, "How would you feel walking around in a foreign country with a false passport?"

It was a strange question, considering that Harel knew Shalom rarely left Israel with anything *other than* a false passport.

"I'd feel fine," Shalom said.

"Fine? You can do that?"

For some reason, Shalom thought, Harel was reluctant to give him his new orders.

"Yes, of course," he replied.

"We're going after Eichmann," said Harel, "and maybe this time we'll get him."

"Give me some details."

"Aharoni has them. Go see him and ask what he found. Then find Rafi. We have to assemble a team."

Shalom went to the Shin Bet offices, in a dilapidated building by the clock tower in Jaffa, to meet Rafi Eitan and draw up a list of people for their operation team.

The first choice was obvious: Shalom Dani, the forger. Dani had escaped from a Nazi concentration camp by making a pass out of toilet paper. They would need his remarkable skills for all the identification documents required. Second was Moshe Tabor. Tabor was not only a strongman — he stood at 6 feet 2, and his hands were the size of baseball mitts — but also a technical master who could create suitcases with false bottoms, overhaul a car engine, fix a submachine gun, pick any lock, and build a safe room that would never, ever, be found.

Harel wanted Zvi Aharoni on the team. His knowledge of the area would be useful, as would his skills as an interrogator. They also agreed on Yaakov Gat, an experienced, cool-headed agent. Eitan pushed for Peter Malkin, another strongman, who had a fine operational mind and who was an expert in disguises. Ephraim Ilani had an encyclopedic knowledge of Buenos Aires and was fluent in Spanish. Dr. Yonah Elian, a civilian anesthesiologist, would keep Eichmann in good health and, if necessary, under sedation. He could also treat any injuries the team might suffer.

Finally, Yaakov Medad would be the front man — the one who arranged the cars, the safe houses, and anything that meant being in the public eye. He was well suited for the job. Medad took to accents easily, remembered background information to the letter, and was able to assume a range of identities and switch back and forth between them at a moment's notice. Most significantly, he had the kind of unassuming, innocent looks that won a stranger's trust in an instant.

It was a good team. Each member had almost a decade of experience in the Israeli intelligence services. They spoke a wide range of languages — key to keeping their cover. Apart from the doctor, they all knew one another extremely well and had worked together on numerous assignments. They understood one another's strengths and weaknesses, could communicate without speaking, and, most important of all, had absolute trust in one another.

Rafi Eitan, Shin Bet Chief of Operations.

Avraham Shalom, Deputy Head of Operations for Shin Bet.

Shalom Dani, forger.

Moshe Tabor,
Mossad agent.

Yaakov Gat,
Mossad agent.

Peter Malkin,
Shin Bet agent.

Yaakov Medad,
Mossad agent.

The Mossad staff began the complicated preparations. It was important that no agent could be tied to another or tracked back to Israel, so all of the agents needed to travel on separate flights, departing from different locations, with forged passports and an array of visas. The visas were a particular challenge, since the Argentine consulate in each country required character references and health documentation before they would issue permission for a foreigner to enter Argentina. Most of this documentation had to be forged. Mossad and Shin Bet staff were sent to Paris to undergo inoculations and medical examinations so that their stamped forms could then be altered and pasted into the forged passports. With all of these preparations, the Mossad headquarters became a veritable travel agency, and staff filled a book the size of a telephone directory with the matrix of identities, flights, and scheduled meeting points.

Any equipment that could not be bought in Argentina without raising suspicion had to be transported in advance using "diplomatic pouch" — a term for any marked container that had immunity from search or seizure because it was sent as part of a country's diplomatic mission. Some of the items Eitan requested included handcuffs, hidden cameras, sedation drugs, miniature drills and woodworking tools, lock picks, field glasses, pocket flashlights, a forgery kit, and a makeup kit with false teeth and wigs. The sizable amount of money needed for the operation was also transported via pouch.

Harel sent Aharoni and Amos Manor, the Shin Bet Director, to Jerusalem to meet with Haim Cohen and Pinhas Rosen, the Israeli Minister of Justice. As the Israeli government's two top lawyers, Cohen and Rosen gave their approval for the mission. It was clear that capturing Eichmann would violate Argentine sovereignty, as one country cannot arrest the citizens of another country without a formal extradition process. But that would be a minor diplomatic issue between the two countries. In their legal opinion, the abduction would not affect Israel's right to prosecute Eichmann, because, they believed, Germany was never going to pursue extradition seriously, let alone hold a trial.

Early on the morning of April 16, the team gathered for the first time, at Shin Bet headquarters in Jaffa. Ephraim Ilani had made the trip from Argentina. Only Yaakov Gat and Dr. Elian were not present. The shades were drawn on the balcony that overlooked the harbor, and Moshe Tabor turned on the slide projector. Aharoni walked them through a comparison of the photographs of Eichmann in his thirties wearing his SS uniform and the shots he had obtained in Argentina.

"Run two of them together," Peter Malkin asked.

Tabor arranged two slides in the projector and put the images up on the blank wall. If they were both Eichmann, Malkin was shocked at how haggard and aged the Nazi had become since the end of the war. "It's not easy to tell, is it?"

"We can't be one hundred percent sure until we've got him," Eitan said.

"Once we're sure," Tabor said, his massive frame a dark silhouette at the back of the room, "why don't we kill the bastard on the spot?"

"We all share that feeling, I'm sure," Eitan said.

Tabor shook his head. He was Lithuanian, and his family had been killed during the Holocaust. He had seen the extermination camps at the end of the war. Revolted and enraged, he had joined a Jewish avenger group and had hunted down, interrogated, and executed numerous SS men. There was no question in any of the team members' minds that he would gladly kill Eichmann himself if given the chance.

Over the next few hours, and during several follow-up meetings, the team ironed out the operational details. Ephraim Ilani briefed them on Argentine local customs — everything from traffic conditions, airport procedures, and styles of dress to how to rent a car or a house and how to behave at a café. Since only Ilani and Aharoni had been to Buenos Aires, and the team wanted to blend in as much as possible, this was key information.

Most of their time was spent planning how and where they would seize Eichmann. They settled on three possible methods. The first was snatching him while he was away from home. The second was a commando raid at night, taking him from his bed. The third involved grabbing him on the street near his house — a possibility given the desolate neighborhood. They'd make a final decision once they were on the ground in Buenos Aires.

Each night, Peter Malkin returned to his Tel Aviv apartment and read, then reread, the Eichmann file. Malkin had broad shoulders like a linebacker and a head like a bowling ball. His expressive, youthful face switched easily from a pensive scowl to almost clownish mirth. Now, though, the Shin Bet agent could only think of his older sister, Fruma, who had stayed behind in Poland in 1933 when the rest of her family emigrated to Palestine. She had died with her husband and three children in the Holocaust.

Malkin knew that because of his strength and speed, he would likely be the one who would actually grab Eichmann. For the first time in his thirty-three years, many of them spent in dangerous situations, he had a profound fear of failure. He focused his every waking moment on the mission ahead and spent hours crafting different disguises and practicing the exact moves needed to overpower his quarry.

With the capture plans coming together, Harel turned his attention to getting Eichmann back to Israel once he had been captured. He had already contacted Yehuda Shimoni, the manager of the Israeli national airline, El Al, to discuss the possibility of sending a plane to Argentina, where the airline did not usually fly. International flights were a much more difficult and dangerous business in 1960, especially when they involved crossing an ocean, but Shimoni assured Harel that it was technically possible for an El Al plane to reach Buenos Aires.

Fortune shone on the mission when Harel learned that Argentina would be celebrating its 150th anniversary of independence from Spain in late May. Delegations from around the world had been invited to attend the festivities — including a group from Israel. It was the ideal cover for an El Al flight.

● ● ●

"Okay, everyone, let's talk," Harel said, seating himself at the desk in his office. His secretary stubbed out her cigarette, leaving one last trail of smoke to dissipate into the air, and placed a stenographer's pad on her lap. The small office was crowded with the key members of the Eichmann operation: Rafi Eitan, Avraham Shalom, Zvi Aharoni, Peter Malkin, Ephraim Ilani, Shalom Dani, and Moshe Tabor. Only Yaakov Gat, who was still in Paris, was absent.

"I want to begin by speaking to you from my heart," Harel said after taking a deep breath. "This is a national mission of the first degree. It is not an ordinary capture operation, but the capture of a hideous Nazi criminal, the most horrible enemy of the Jewish people. We are not performing this operation as adventurers but as representatives of the Jewish people and the state of Israel. Our objective is to bring Eichmann back safely, fully in good health, so he can be put to trial.

"There might well be difficult repercussions. We know this. We have not only the right but also the moral duty to bring this man to trial. You must remember this throughout the weeks ahead. You are guardian angels of justice, the emissaries of the Jewish people."

The men looked at one another as Harel spoke. They knew that he had dedicated his life to Israel and that everything he did was a matter of principle, but on this day he was particularly fervent and eloquent, and his words stirred his team.

"We will bring Adolf Eichmann to Jerusalem," Harel said, "and perhaps the world will be reminded of its responsibilities. It will be recognized that, as a people, we never forgot. Our memory reaches back through recorded history. The memory book lies open, and the hand still writes."

He turned to Eitan. "Are your people ready?" he asked, his tone cool, no longer layered with feeling.

"All ready," Eitan replied.

CHAPTER 8

On April 24, Yaakov Gat flew into Ezeiza Airport, Buenos Aires. Born in Transylvania, a region of Romania, Gat had a personal stake in the operation to find Eichmann: Many in his extended family had been sent to extermination camps by the Nazis. Dressed in an immaculately cut suit, his suitcase in hand, Gat smoothly managed passport control despite his lack of Spanish. Then he stepped out of the plane into the harsh glare of the Argentine sun. Instead of taking a taxi, whose driver might later remember where he had dropped off his passenger, he boarded a bus outside the terminal. He was scheduled to meet Ephraim Ilani in a couple of hours. He took a seat close to the doorway, as was his habit, just in case there was a problem.

The bus to the city center was jammed with people, but there was no sign of the driver. A policeman was walking around the front of the bus. After ten minutes, no driver in sight, Gat began to worry. After twenty, he was convinced that something was terribly wrong.

Suddenly, two men rushed onto the bus, blocking the exit. Gat figured that one was the driver, because of his uniform. The other placed himself directly in front of Gat and rattled off something in Spanish. Gat froze.

The man showed him a photograph of himself in profile coming off the plane. Questions rushed through Gat's mind. Did the Argentine police know who he was? Had they been tipped off?

Did they know his passport was fake? Was he about to be detained?

Before he could react, the man turned to the next passenger and presented *him* with a freshly developed picture of himself. It dawned on Gat that the man was just a photographer, hoping to cash in on some tourist business. He obviously had an arrangement with the bus company and the police to hold the bus until he had developed his photos.

When the man came back around, Gat gladly paid for the picture and then eased himself back in his seat. If he had made a run for it and had been caught, he might have compromised the entire mission before it began. Such were the dangers from even the most harmless of incidents.

At eleven o'clock, Gat walked into a café in the center of Buenos Aires. Ephraim Ilani was waiting for him there, a cup of coffee in his hand and a pipe in his mouth. Twice a day he had gone to a prearranged street corner, restaurant, or café — a different rendezvous each time to avoid suspicion — expecting to meet with one of the operations team. He never knew who might arrive or on what day.

"Pleased to see you! Come, sit here!" Ilani said joyfully in English, sliding out of the booth seat.

"How are you?" Gat asked brightly in the same language, projecting his voice. "I've come straight from the airport."

Later, they spoke quietly in Hebrew, then left the café to visit the safe house Ilani had found and equipped.

The next day, Zvi Aharoni met them in a similar manner at a restaurant. Since his last trip to Buenos Aires earlier in the month, Aharoni had let his hair grow out and now sported a mustache to avoid being recognized by anyone with whom he'd had contact on the previous visit.

Avraham Shalom was next to arrive. He had flown to Rome under one passport, switching it for another at the Israeli Embassy. Then he traveled by train to Paris, where Shalom Dani gave him an authentic German passport whose name he had carefully changed by a few letters. He had then flown to Lisbon.

Shalom had to surrender his forged passport to the Portuguese authorities until just before boarding his flight to Buenos Aires. Inexplicably, he forgot his assumed name when the policeman holding the pile of passengers' passports asked him for it. Usually he used some kind of mnemonic device to remember his cover names, linking syllables or letters of the first name with the last, but this time his mind was struck blank. Luckily, he spotted his green passport in the pile and pointed to it, saying confidently, "That one's mine." The policeman handed it to him without a problem.

When Shalom arrived at the reception desk of his hotel in Buenos Aires, he gave his passport to the receptionist. The man took one look at his papers and said, "Compatriot. You're from Hamburg. I'm from Hamburg!"

Shalom felt his limbs go weak. He was originally from Vienna and spoke German with an Austrian accent. The receptionist would surely notice that he did not speak like a German from the north. What was more, the man's age and nationality were consistent with the possibility that he might have been a Nazi. Aiming to put him off, Shalom said that he was actually from a small town outside the city. The receptionist replied that *he* was from the same place. Shalom was stunned. What were the chances?! He made haste with the hotel forms, took the keys to his room, and walked away, certain that he had made a poor impression. He would have to change hotels.

The team members had scheduled a 6:00 P.M. rendezvous at the corner of Avenida Santa Fe and Avenida Callao. Shalom arrived at the same time as Aharoni and Gat.

"What do you want to do, Avrum?" Aharoni asked, deferring to Shalom as the Shin Bet deputy director.

"Let's go to his house," Shalom decided. "No reason to delay."

"It'll be dark," Aharoni said.

"We'll go."

By the time they reached San Fernando by car, the sun had set, and a slight mist hung in the cool evening air. The lack of streetlights in the area was proof of its isolation. As they passed under the railway embankment on Route 202, Shalom saw small, alternating red and white lights up ahead and to his right. Soon he realized it was a person walking with a double-headed flashlight. When the car's headlights lit up the pedestrian's face, Shalom recognized Eichmann.

"That's him! That's the man," Shalom said sharply.

Aharoni braked and steered to the side of the road, as if he expected Shalom and Gat to jump out and grab Eichmann straightaway.

"Stop that! Drive away!" Shalom said. "He'll think that something's wrong."

Aharoni hit the accelerator and steered the car back onto the road, too horrified at his mistake to utter a word. Gat watched from the backseat, praying Eichmann would not turn around to see what had caused the car to slow down and veer right. Thankfully, he did not.

They continued for a few hundred feet down Route 202 before Shalom instructed Aharoni to stop.

"Gat, go after him and see if it's Eichmann," Shalom said.

Gat jumped out and crossed the street, keeping one hundred yards between himself and the man. The lights from the car disappeared, and the neighborhood was shrouded in darkness. He watched the red and white lights move sharply to the left and knew that the man must have turned onto Garibaldi Street. He followed. The man walked twenty yards farther before angling toward a pillbox of a house — one that matched the photographs Aharoni had taken.

A half hour later, Aharoni picked up Gat on the opposite side of the embankment.

"Eichmann," Gat said. He was excited that they had found their target on the first night.

Shalom thought that he had seen enough to cable Harel. It was a Tuesday, and Eichmann was probably returning from work, having taken the bus. If this turned out to be the case, then it was possible that Eichmann returned home at the same time every day and walked along an empty, dark street to a house in an unlit, isolated neighborhood. It didn't get any better for a capture operation, thought Shalom.

Early the next morning, April 27, Shalom met with Ephraim Ilani, the only member of the team working out of the Israeli embassy. He passed him a single code word to send to Tel Aviv: "Carrot" — the mission should move forward.

When he received the message later that day, Harel called Rafi Eitan and gave him the nod for the rest of the team to travel to Buenos Aires. With the mission now going ahead, Harel hurried to finalize the plans for Eichmann's transport out of

Argentina. He had already chosen the date when the special El Al flight would leave Tel Aviv for Argentina: May 11. This would allow the Foreign Ministry delegation to arrive a week before the anniversary celebrations in Argentina, and it met with El Al's scheduling demands.

Harel met with chief pilot Zvi Tohar and the two men charged with selecting and vetting the crew: El Al Security Officer Adi Peleg and Head of Crew Assignments Baruch Tirosh. "Look, friends, this is the situation," Harel began, gravely serious. "We have a flight to carry an Israeli delegation to the Argentine anniversary. On the return journey, we will be bringing Adolf Eichmann back with us."

The three men listened intently as Harel detailed his plan. He wanted only Israelis selected for the flight, cabin, and ground

Captain Zvi Tohar, El Al.

crews. They were to be trustworthy and extremely capable. Every technical detail was to be treated with extra care. The flight crew would need to be ready to take off quickly from Buenos Aires and, potentially, to make evasive maneuvers if they were pursued by Argentine fighter planes. "What do you have to say about this?" Harel asked.

Tirosh affirmed that they could handle the assignment, but said that, given the distance, they would need two full crews. He suggested that they might throw off potential pursuers by filing a false flight plan for the return journey.

Peleg was noticeably moved by the prospect of the mission. Shortly after the Nazis had come to power in Germany, his father, a successful merchant, had been beaten and forced to drink liters of castor oil. Soon after that, he had died of a heart attack.

Harel stressed that he wanted to limit the number of stops on the return flight from Buenos Aires. Normally, three stops for refueling would be required for a journey of that distance — for example, one in Recife, Brazil; a second in Dakar, Senegal, on the other side of the Atlantic Ocean; and a third in Rome, Italy, before the plane crossed the Mediterranean to Tel Aviv. Harel felt that this would provide too many opportunities for the plane to be seized should their mission be exposed.

"Will you be able to manage with only one stop?" he asked.

"It is a very long flight," Tohar said. "Let me check it out."

Two hours later, he rang Harel to tell him that a flight with only one stop, in Dakar, was possible at a level of risk he was willing to take. But there could be no guarantees. At some point over the Atlantic Ocean, they would pass the point of no return.

• • •

Lying flat on their stomachs at the top of the railway embankment, their faces inches from the tracks, Shalom and Aharoni trained their binoculars on Route 202 and on the house seventy-five yards away. This was the third night they had watched Eichmann walk home.

Lights appeared on the road. Aharoni checked his watch: 7:38 P.M. On the previous two nights, at 7:40, the green and yellow No. 203 bus had stopped at the kiosk, and Eichmann had stepped off. They had his schedule down. Their whole operation would depend on his sticking to it.

Tonight, again, Eichmann stepped off of the bus. After it moved away, he turned on his flashlight and walked slowly, head down, toward his house.

Avraham Shalom had been struck by Eichmann's impoverished existence. He lived in a shabby neighborhood, without electricity or running water, and dressed in the threadbare clothes of a simple factory worker. Given the power Eichmann had once held, it was hard for Shalom to believe that this was the same man.

Shalom and Aharoni watched the house for a few more minutes. Then they descended the embankment, where Gat picked them up at a prearranged time. The three men returned to the safe house, a grand second-floor apartment in an exclusive neighborhood. They had dubbed the place Maoz, which means "stronghold" in Hebrew. They needed to find another safe house in which to keep Eichmann, one with very specific requirements: It had to be a large house in a fairly wealthy area so that several expensive cars could be seen coming and going without arousing suspicion. It had to be private, therefore detached, and preferably have a fenced garden and an attached garage so they could bring their prisoner directly inside without anyone seeing him. Finally, the location had to be remote — but not too far from either San Fernando or the airport — and accessible by a variety of routes. In the best case, they would rent a house from a local Jew, explaining that they wanted to use it for the Israeli diplomatic delegation. Then, if circumstances demanded, they could call on their landlord to turn a blind eye.

The team decided to split into two groups and spend all of the next day checking out suitable locations.

●●●

"The initial team has located Eichmann and reported good chances for the operation." Harel was standing across from David Ben-Gurion in the Prime Minister's office.

"Are you certain that the man is Adolf Eichmann?" Ben-Gurion asked.

The Mossad chief listed his reasons, although he had come to see Ben-Gurion to ask for his farewell blessing, not to be quizzed. Harel was scheduled to depart for Buenos Aires the following day, and Ben-Gurion was hesitant about him joining the task force. Having an intelligence agent caught on foreign soil would be a problem; having the chief of Israel's security services caught on foreign soil would be a disaster. Harel understood this, but he wanted to be on the ground in Buenos Aires to make sure that everything went well. He felt that the mission was too important and too complicated to be trusted to someone else.

Israeli Prime Minister David Ben-Gurion in 1948.

Once again he explained to Ben-Gurion his reasons for join-ing the team, and the Prime Minister assented, asking only how long he would be.

"Three to four weeks," Harel estimated.

Ben-Gurion came around his desk and shook Harel's hand. "Dead or alive, just bring Eichmann back with you," he said. His brow furrowed as he reflected on this. "Preferably alive. It would be very important, morally, for the young generations of Israel."

CHAPTER 9

Shalom and Gat spent Sunday, May 1, driving around San Fernando in an old Chevrolet, testing every possible route for the night they would capture Eichmann. Streetcar crossings were a particular problem for a clean getaway: In many areas, one could not drive for more than a few blocks without having to stop to wait for a streetcar to pass and the barrier to lift.

Their own cars were another issue. There were very few new vehicles in Argentina because of the struggling economy. Rentals were expensive, difficult to find, and utterly undependable. Each time Yaakov Medad rented a car, he had to show ID and put down a large security deposit (sometimes as much as $5,000), which risked arousing suspicion and exposing the Israelis' presence in the country. Yet they were going to need a pair of reliable large sedans — a rare breed of vehicle in Argentina — for the capture itself.

Isser Harel arrived in Buenos Aires later that day and met with his team at Maoz in the evening. Shalom detailed what they had learned from their surveillance. Harel listened closely, occasionally nodding his head. He agreed that Eichmann's strict routine and isolated neighborhood were ideal for the operation.

Then he told them about the preparations for the El Al flight. Since the plane was scheduled to leave Israel on May 11 and to depart from Buenos Aires on May 14, their window to capture Eichmann would be a narrow one.

Yosef Klein, the manager of El Al's base in New York's Idlewild Airport (now John F. Kennedy Airport), could not work out why El Al headquarters wanted him to fly to Argentina — or why it had to be immediately. But that was what the telex message said: "Go to Buenos Aires. Meet up with Yehuda Shimoni. Arrive by May 3." He expected that they would be putting together some kind of charter flight.

Klein flew first class with Swissair to Rio de Janeiro, arriving on May 2 for his connecting flight to Argentina. The trip was going to be an enjoyable, relaxing jaunt, he had decided. The thirty-year-old bachelor planned to have some fun and to visit the newly built city of Brasília, about to be inaugurated as Brazil's capital.

In the first-class cabin, he met Yehuda Shimoni, the manager of El Al. They exchanged greetings and sat down together. Klein

Yosef Klein, El Al.

noticed that Shimoni, whom he had known since joining El Al in 1952, was unusually tense and asked him if anything was wrong.

Shimoni shifted in his seat and spoke quietly. "We have a major assignment. There is likely one of the Nazi strongmen who escaped from Europe in Buenos Aires. The Israeli secret services suspect that they have located him, and they are following him. There's a good chance that he is the right man. If they do get hold of him, it will be our job to get him out of Argentina and into Israel. And for this purpose, there will be a special flight, under certain covers."

Klein could hardly believe what he had just been told. He was too shocked to say anything more than "We'll do it, if it's possible."

Shimoni then explained that it was Adolf Eichmann they were after and what the Nazi officer had done during the war. Klein remained silent, and Shimoni reassured him that his job had nothing to do with catching Eichmann. He was there simply to look after the flight.

For a while, the two sat quietly as Klein was overcome by memories of the past. He had been in Auschwitz with his family: The guards had separated him and his father from his mother and younger brother and sister, who were sent immediately to the gas chambers. His father had said that Yosef was seventeen, not fourteen, and this had saved his life.

Later that night, after they landed, Klein and Shimoni sat down with Isser Harel in a café in the city. Shimoni would be leaving in a few days, and then Klein would be on his own.

"What your job entails," Harel told him, "is to make all the arrangements for the flight." Even though Klein did not speak

Spanish or know the airport, he would be responsible for everything associated with the plane from its arrival to its departure. He needed to establish good relations with all the relevant Argentine ministries, as well as with the service companies and other airlines that would be accommodating El Al, which had no infrastructure in the country. Furthermore, Harel wanted Klein to survey the airport, its facilities, and its customs and passport procedures and recommend the best way to get their prisoner on board the plane.

"We're not here just to do a job," he said, sensing that Klein needed some encouragement. "This is the first time the Jewish people will judge their murderer."

●●●

On May 3, Yaakov Gat spent yet another morning in a café, expecting Peter Malkin and Rafi Eitan to come through the door. Yet again they failed to show. They were late arriving in Buenos Aires, he thought — too late. Moshe Tabor, who had landed the day before, had met with them in Paris, but he did not know the reason for their delay. If they had been caught attempting to get into Argentina with false passports, then Ephraim Ilani, at the embassy, had yet to receive word.

In their absence, the rest of the team continued their surveillance of Eichmann, shadowing his movements to and from his job at a car factory to see if there was a better spot to snatch him than outside his home. They forged ahead with their search for suitable safe houses, and, after forty-eight hours of intensive work, their efforts were rewarded with two buildings.

The first was in the quiet neighborhood of Florencio Varela, eighteen miles southwest of Buenos Aires. The large two-story house, code-named Tira ("palace"), had several advantages: easy access to both the capture area and the airport, an eight-foot-high perimeter wall, a gated entrance, no caretaker, and a garden and veranda shielded from view by trees and dense shrubs. It was by no means perfect. There were neighbors on both sides, and the house lacked an attic or basement in which to hide the prisoner. Still, it was a good backup for the other property.

This second and better villa, code-named Doron ("gift"), was only a couple of hours from Garibaldi Street, and there were several routes into the area. The extensive manicured grounds were surrounded by a high stone wall. The only drawback was that there was a gardener, but the team felt confident that he could be persuaded to stay away. This was where they would hold Eichmann until it was time to bring him to the airport.

● ● ●

After their first day's work in Buenos Aires, Shimoni and Klein of El Al again met with Harel at a café. One look at their faces told Harel there was a problem. Shimoni explained that the Argentine protocol office was not prepared to welcome the Israeli delegation before May 19, a week later than they had expected. There was no way to negotiate with them without drawing too much attention to the flight.

Harel considered the options. They would have to either postpone the capture or risk holding Eichmann for ten days until the plane could take off on May 20. Neither was a good choice. Delaying increased the chances that Eichmann would change his routine or, much worse, that he would discover he was being watched and run. Extending his imprisonment in the safe house gave anyone who would be looking for him — his family, the police, or both — more time to find him.

After the El Al officers left, Shalom joined Harel at his café table. Shalom suggested they postpone the operation by at least a few days. Harel feared that even this minor delay would give Eichmann a chance to evade capture. Needing time to think — and hoping to discuss the situation further with Rafi Eitan, if and when he arrived — he put off making a decision. One thing was certain: The news increased the risks for everyone involved.

On the evening of May 4, Rafi Eitan and Peter Malkin finally appeared at their meeting place. They had been held up in Paris with documentation problems and a case of food poisoning. Shalom collected them in a 1952 Ford clunker. With the operation only six days away, they wanted to go straight to San Fernando.

As they drove north, a light rain fell and a cold, blustery wind picked up. By the time they neared Eichmann's neighborhood, the drizzle had turned into a downpour, but Malkin still recognized some of the landmarks and streets he had studied in Aharoni's reports.

Suddenly, on a street parallel to Garibaldi, two young soldiers materialized, one on either side of the vehicle. Shalom stopped the car abruptly. He stayed calm; he had run across enough roadblocks and spot-checks to know that this was routine for Buenos Aires. In his pidgin Spanish he explained to one of the soldiers that they were tourists looking for their hotel. The soldier did not reply, shining his flashlight first on Shalom, then on the license plate. Rain streamed off the brim of his hat as he contemplated whether they were a threat. After an age, he waved them on, to the relief of the three Israelis.

A few blocks away, Shalom pulled over to the side of the road. "We'd better leave the car here. I'd hate for those soldiers to see it again."

They exited the car and within moments were drenched from head to foot in the downpour. Malkin hiked across a muddy field in the dark, cursing his suit and dress shoes. But when he reached the lookout post on the railway embankment, he forgot about everything except the house on which his binoculars were now trained. The post was perfectly positioned, and Malkin was able to see Eichmann's wife clearly through the front window. He checked his watch. According to Shalom, Eichmann would arrive within the next few minutes.

His hands numb from the cold and rain, Malkin held the binoculars up to his face again. He saw a bus approach down Route 202. It stopped at the kiosk, and a man in a trench coat and hat got off.

"That's him," Shalom whispered.

The sight of the lone figure walking through the driving rain burned in Malkin's mind: This was the man he had come to Argentina to capture. He was already calculating the type of takedown he would use and where on the stretch of road he would make his move.

What none of the three men knew was that Zvi Aharoni had traveled part of the way with Eichmann that night. In an attempt to work out where Eichmann boarded bus 203, Aharoni had gone to the station in Carupa, eight stops from San Fernando, dressed in worker's overalls. As he boarded the old green and yellow bus, which was thronged with factory workers and secretaries, he saw Eichmann sitting halfway down. Aharoni looked away so as not to be caught staring and handed the driver four

Surveyors' map of Garibaldi Street used by the capture team.

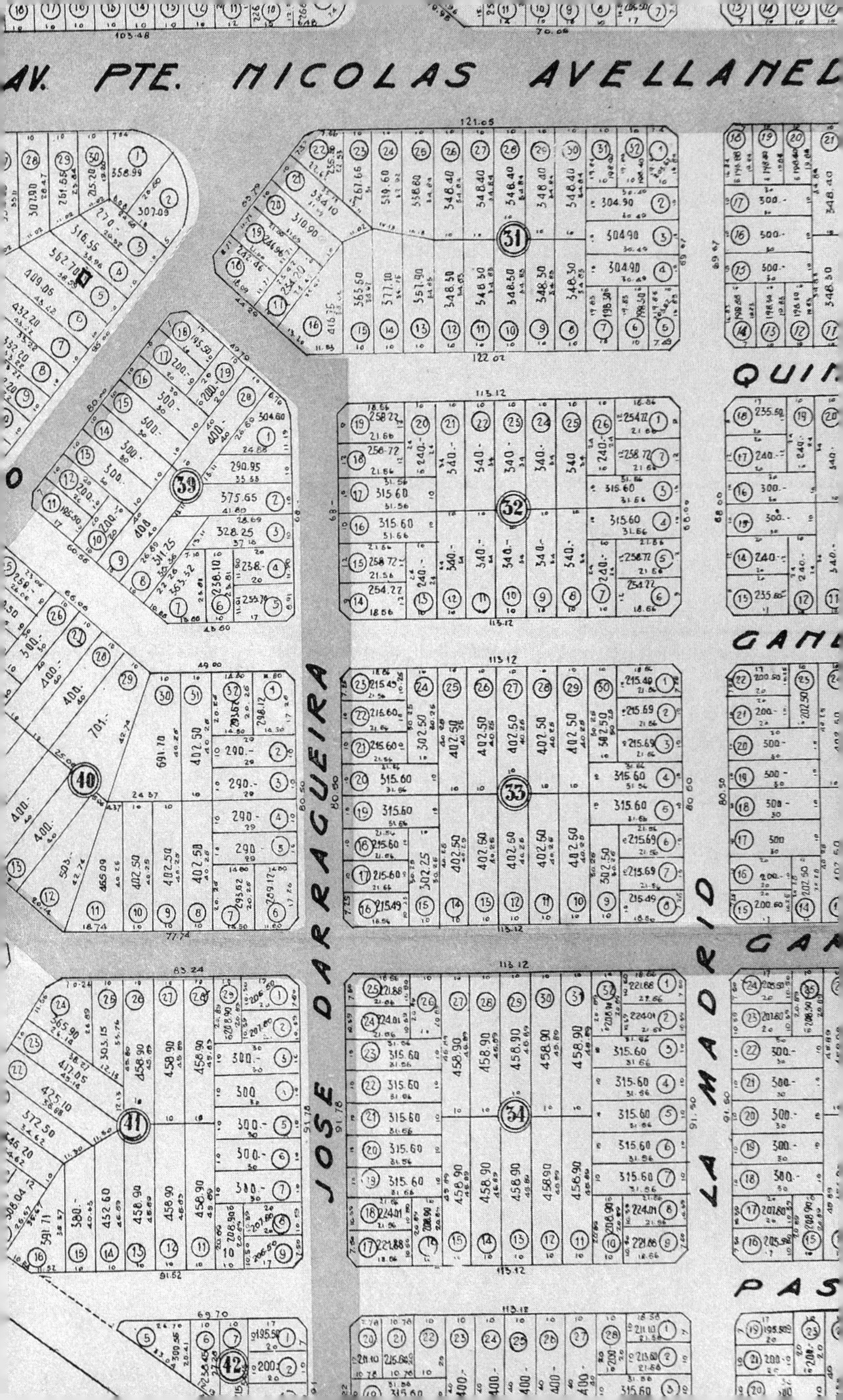

AV. PTE. NICOLAS AVELLANED

QUIN...

GAN...

GAN...

PAS...

JOSE DARRAGUEIRA

LA MADRID

31

32

33

34

39

40

41

42

pesos for a ticket. If the driver asked him a question in Spanish, Aharoni would surely draw attention to himself. Fortunately, he did not.

Walking down the aisle, Aharoni realized that the only empty seat was directly behind Eichmann, who was oblivious to him as he passed. He slid into the seat, barely noticing the steel springs that jutted through the worn leather. He was close enough to reach out and put his hands around Eichmann's neck.

As the bus shuddered to a start, Aharoni felt a rush of emotion that left him physically weak. Severely distressed, he could not wait to get off at the San Fernando station. If there was ever any doubt in his mind that they were after more than just a man, this brief encounter dispelled that doubt. He felt they were closing in on evil itself.

The next day, Rafi Eitan instructed everyone to meet at Maoz. In the living room of the apartment, the agents ran through everything they had learned. It was clear from all their surveillance that they should capture Eichmann on his walk home. They discussed the numerous possible variations of carrying out the abduction and agreed that they should get him as soon as he turned onto Garibaldi Street, away from any passing traffic.

As for the date of the operation, they had all heard that the El Al flight was not due now until May 19. Eitan made it clear that Isser Harel had decided there would be no delay. It was better to risk holding Eichmann for longer than first planned than to let him slip through their fingers. May 10 was now the date, just five short days away.

CHAPTER 10

At Ezeiza Airport, Yosef Klein was organizing the return flight. He had met with officials at Aerolíneas Argentinas, the national airline, and at TransAer, a private local airline that flew the same planes, Britannias, as did El Al. He had also taken care to befriend everyone from the baggage handlers, customs officers, and policemen to the service crews, maintenance workers, and staffs of both airlines. He intimated that this diplomatic flight might be a test run for a regular El Al service to Argentina. The potential to earn higher wages with El Al made everyone eager to help.

Thanks to all his research, Klein had concluded that Eichmann could not be brought onto the plane through the terminal building. There were too many customs and immigration officers, and little escaped their attention. He needed to find a place to park the El Al plane that would allow the Mossad to get their prisoner on board.

The TransAer hangar was the ideal spot, located at the edge of the airfield, where there were fewer guards. Since the airline flew Britannias, Klein could easily say that El Al wanted to park its plane there, should any spare parts or special maintenance be required.

Back at Maoz, on the evening of May 5, Shalom Dani had arrived carrying several suitcases and boxes labeled FRAGILE. He immediately got to work forging documents. At just thirty-two years of age, Dani suffered from heart problems, but he was determined to be in on this job. When the Nazis occupied Hungary, his family had been moved from their village into a ghetto. His father had been killed at Bergen-Belsen, and Dani, his two siblings, and their mother had been shuffled among various camps until he crafted the passes that freed them.

Now, in his left hand, Dani held a magnifying glass. With his steady right hand he fashioned a typewriter-perfect letter *E* with a fine-tipped black pen. The table in front of him was covered with colored pens and pencils, inks, dyes, small brushes, knives, clumps of wax, a hot plate, seals, cameras, film, bottles of photographic developer, and paper in every color and weight imaginable. He needed to create dozens of different passports, driver's licenses, insurance cards, IDs, and other papers for the team.

Moshe Tabor likewise worked alone throughout the days that followed. He punched out a number of sets of fake license plates for the capture cars and rigged a system to change them in seconds. These included a set of diplomatic plates. He also tinkered with a contraption to turn the backseat of the car into a trapdoor, which would allow them to hide Eichmann in the narrow space between the trunk and the seat if necessary.

Meanwhile, Avraham Shalom mapped out three separate routes to each safe house, with backups in case a road was blocked or they were followed. He also assisted Medad and Ilani with the search for suitable capture cars. Eventually, they found a black Buick limousine, only four years old, and a large Chevrolet sedan. It needed work, but Tabor could overhaul an engine as easily as winding a watch.

Even more work was required to prepare for the prisoner's arrival at Doron. The team stocked the house with beds and

Moshe Tabor's kit for making false license plates.

food, as well as all the equipment they had brought from Israel. They reinforced the security bars on the windows and changed the locks. Tabor surveyed the house and found a spot in the attic where they could hide the prisoner in case of a search. He moved some support beams slightly and built a false wall that opened on a hinge. The casual observer would never know it was there.

Repeated, sometimes painful, rehearsals of the snatch were held in the garage at Doron. One agent would play Eichmann, walking down the street. Malkin or Tabor would grab him, and two others would help get him into the car. Eitan wanted this action down to fewer than twelve seconds, not giving Eichmann the chance even to scream. The team practiced ten to twenty times a night, each of them wanting the movements to become second nature.

Throughout all this, the surveillance of Eichmann continued, despite the risks it posed. Malkin wanted to know every one of Eichmann's movements from the bus stop to his house, going so far as to count the number of strides he took to get there. Day after day, their target showed up at exactly the same time. He was in their sights.

On May 8, a bitterly cold Sunday, Eitan and Shalom met the team's doctor at a designated spot in Buenos Aires. In his early forties, of medium height, and wearing a sharp, expensive suit, Yonah Elian looked very much at ease, although he was traveling with false papers on a mission that could land him in an Argentine jail if things went badly. It was not the first time the Israeli secret service had called on him, but, because he was a Holocaust survivor, this mission was special.

Dr. Yonah Elian

They brought Elian to Doron, where he was introduced to Tabor and Malkin. "We're glad you're here," Malkin said, shivering in the freezing room. "I hope you've had some experience with treating double pneumonia."

"Oh, I understood this to be a vacation." The doctor grinned. "I thought I only had one patient to worry about."

They liked him immediately.

In the city, Isser Harel actually *was* ill. The stress of the operation and his constant movement among eight to twelve cafés a day had left him with a fever and a thick cold. Nevertheless, this was no time to rest.

That night, Rafi Eitan gathered the operations team together at Doron. A hand-drawn map was pinned to the wall. A broken blue line showed the path Eichmann took each day from the bus stop to his house. Bus 203's route through the area was designated with a solid green line, and the surrounding streets were solid red. Key landmarks, including the railway embankment and the kiosk, were also detailed. A black X indicated the Eichmann house.

Aharoni outlined the plan. The Chevrolet would be stationed on Route 202. It would turn on its lights in order to blind Eichmann as he walked toward them. The Buick would be parked on Garibaldi Street, facing away from Route 202, with its hood up, as if it had broken down. As Eichmann drew near to the Buick, Malkin would say something to him in Spanish to distract him before grabbing him. Then Tabor and Eitan would help drag him into the backseat.

The plan decided, the team turned to the next issue. The gardener at Doron was a simple, gentle man, but he was suspicious about all the activity at the house. He was on the premises too often and could not be persuaded to stay away. One mention of the strange activities to the wrong person could compromise the whole operation. Everyone agreed without question that they must switch safe houses and keep Eichmann at Tira instead.

On May 9, driving to San Fernando on reconnaissance, Rafi Eitan turned onto Route 202 near Garibaldi Street, and suddenly found himself at the scene of an accident. A car had smashed into a motorcycle. Before Eitan could turn around, a policeman stepped up to his window with the bloodied motorcyclist. "Hospital," the policeman said.

There was nothing for Eitan to do but nod enthusiastically and drive off with the man to get him medical treatment.

The incident decided him on an issue that he'd been turning over in his mind for some time. He sat down with Harel later that morning and announced that they should postpone the capture by a day. He had doubted that the team would be ready when they had decided they needed to move safe houses. But now, because of the incident with the police, he was certain: He did not want to risk being seen in the area two days in a row.

Harel was reluctant, but he agreed. They would delay the capture until May 11.

• • •

"We're planning for the operation to take place tomorrow," Harel told Yosef Klein. "So, just be aware of that."

Klein had mapped out the airport for Harel — its every entrance, building, runway, and guard position, as well as the locations of some windows and doors. He had also outlined the routine movements into and out of the airport, as well as staff shift changes. He had learned quickly how Harel liked to do things.

Now Klein told the Mossad chief that when he had gone to TransAer's maintenance area earlier that day, he found soldiers and police everywhere. Whatever the reason, they could no longer use that area to board the plane. He had already selected an alternative: the Aerolíneas Argentinas facilities. Although they were closer to the main terminal, the area was poorly lit at night and guarded by only a few soldiers. What was more, it could be accessed without passing through the entrance to the main terminal.

Harel gave Klein the go-ahead to set it up.

• • •

Even with the one-day reprieve, the team rushed to finish their preparations. They needed to check out of their hotels, move into their assigned safe houses, and assume completely different identities.

At Tira, Moshe Tabor again prepared a space for the prisoner. He had chosen a ten-by-twelve-foot room on the second floor for Eichmann's cell. First he moved a cast-iron bed into the room. Then he secured heavy wool blankets over the two windows and four walls. These would muffle any sounds Eichmann might make. Tabor rigged a bell in the room, an alarm that could be activated from the front gate or the living room if the house was about to be searched. Two separate spaces served as hiding holes, both padded heavily with blankets. One was underneath the veranda, where there was a foot and a half of clearance between the wooden floor and the concrete foundation. The other was in a small storage space above the cell.

In the kitchen, Zvi Aharoni attempted to teach Malkin the few phrases in Spanish he would say to Eichmann to put him at ease before grabbing him. At first they tried, "Can you tell me what time it is?" and then, "Excuse me, please?" but Malkin had unusual difficulty with Spanish. He settled for a simple "*Un momentito, señor*" ("a moment, sir").

Meanwhile, in the garage, Shalom and Gat washed the two capture cars to make them look worthy of their diplomatic status. They continued to practice changing the license plates and testing the hollow space behind the backseat.

They stopped all this activity for one final meeting. Isser Harel stood before his men, and they were silent. "You were chosen by destiny to guarantee that one of the worst criminals of all time, who for years has succeeded in evading justice, would be made to stand trial in Jerusalem," he began, his voice clear. "For the first time in history the Jews will judge their assassins, and for the first time the world will hear the full story of the edict of annihilation against an entire people. Everything depends on the action we are about to take."

Harel then reviewed the capture plan and the responsibilities of each member. From the lead car, the one stationed on Garibaldi Street, Malkin would make the first move on Eichmann, and Tabor would back him up. Aharoni would drive, and Eitan was to remain out of sight, ready to lead the team and assist where necessary. In the second car, parked on Route 202, Shalom would be the driver, Gat would act as lookout, and Dr. Elian would be on hand to administer any medicine required.

Then they talked backup plans. What should they do if they found out that Ricardo Klement was not Adolf Eichmann? This was still a possibility, albeit a faint one. Still, if they discovered that they had made a mistake, Harel instructed Malkin and Tabor to drive Klement several hundred miles north of the city and to drop him off with some money. Then they were to cross over the border into Brazil while the rest of the team got out of Argentina.

What would happen if Eichmann managed to escape and reach his house? Their orders were to break into the house, using whatever means necessary, and to grab him there.

What if the police chased them before they reached the safe house? They were to use every evasive driving maneuver in their repertoire, break every traffic law, and even use the second car, the one driven by Shalom, to ram their pursuers if necessary.

What if they were caught *with* Eichmann? "Under no circumstances whatsoever are we to let him go or allow him to escape," Harel said. As many of the team as possible were to slip away, but Rafi Eitan was to handcuff himself to Eichmann and ask for the ranking Argentine police officer. He would then declare that he was a Jewish volunteer, operating without governmental authority, who had heard that this notorious Nazi war criminal was living in Buenos Aires and wanted him brought to trial. Until he was promised that his captive would be held pending an investigation, Eitan was to do everything possible not to be separated from Eichmann.

Every single member of the team knew the stakes when they began the operation, but hearing what they were to do if they were caught made the risks even more real.

"Are there any questions?" Harel asked.

Thinking of his wife and two children, including a daughter barely six months old, Yaakov Gat asked, "If there's a problem with the authorities, and they arrest us with Eichmann, how long can we expect to sit in jail in Argentina?"

"I checked," Harel replied, surprising no one. "Maximum, ten years. But with diplomatic influence, maybe two or three."

"Who looks after our families?" Gat asked, knowing it was a question the others wanted answered as well.

"I'm responsible," Harel said firmly. "I'm in charge." Not one of the team doubted him. His loyalty to his people was unquestioned.

Harel finished by wishing good luck to every one of them. They were now on their own.

CHAPTER 11

When the Mossad team awoke on May 11, they faced a long day of nervous waiting before they could execute the capture that evening. Tabor and Malkin double-checked that the safe house was ready and finished the hiding places. Shalom, Gat, and Eitan drove to San Fernando and back to check that no obstruction had appeared along the routes. Aharoni made a rushed trip to a garage to buy a new battery for the Buick.

By early afternoon, they had run out of ways to pass the time. Everyone involved in the capture operation waited at Tira. Between games of chess and gin rummy, they looked for anything other than the operation to talk about, but there was no point. Some retired to their rooms to relax — maybe even to sleep — but they were always back in the living room shortly after, more on edge than ever.

An hour before they were due to leave, Malkin splashed some water on his face and pulled on a wig, a blue wool sweater, and black pants. For a long time he stared at himself in the mirror, mentally charging himself up. Memories of his family overran his thoughts, followed by a rush of fear that he might fail his team and, in some way, all the people who had died because of Eichmann, including Fruma, her husband, and their three children. To push these feelings away, he repeated to himself, "I'm going to catch him."

Then he went downstairs to find everyone else was ready. Tabor had also put on a wig, covering his bald head, and he wore a heavy overcoat that made him look even more like a giant than usual. The others had dressed in jackets and slacks. Some wore ties, to look more like diplomats, but they were not in disguise. Only Malkin and Tabor would be outside the car.

Before they left, Eitan reviewed their plan one more time. He offered no eloquent words of inspiration. Each of them knew what he needed to do. It was half past six. Time to go.

● ● ●

Adolf Eichmann began his day as usual, rising from bed before sunrise. He shaved, washed himself in a pail of water, and then had breakfast. He left his house, caught bus 203 at the kiosk, and began his daily two-hour trek to work at a Mercedes-Benz

Eichmann's Mercedes-Benz identity card.

manufacturing plant. He switched buses twice, catching the one for the final leg at Saavedra Bridge, which separated the city center from the outlying districts of Buenos Aires. This bus was filled with the same people every day, mostly his fellow workers. He offered only spare greetings to the other passengers during the twenty-mile ride. Some of them knew his name, Ricardo Klement, but that was about it.

At the plant, he clocked in like everyone else and put on a pair of dark-blue Mercedes-Benz overalls. As a foreman, he spent the morning winding his way up and down the assembly line, checking the work in progress. When the 12:30 P.M. whistle blew, he took his lunch break, alone, in the restaurant at which he ate every working day. An hour later, he returned to work exactly on time, and stayed there until he finished his shift.

● ● ●

Zvi Aharoni turned the Buick limousine off the highway, heading toward Route 202. Rafi Eitan sat beside him, and Tabor and Malkin were in the back. They all kept their eyes trained on the road, though they glanced at one another occasionally. They knew that each of them depended on his teammates for the success of the operation — and, potentially, for his own freedom and even his life.

At 7:35 P.M., they reached Garibaldi Street. Shalom, driving the Chevrolet, had taken a different route, but the two cars arrived at the same time. Gat was in the passenger's seat, at relative ease. He knew they had a good plan. More than that: He had faith in the team.

In the backseat, the doctor was quiet and still. He was looking at the Mossad agents through different eyes. They were almost a separate breed of men, he thought, so calm in the moments before this covert operation began.

In five minutes, the bus would arrive. They had not wanted to be in the area for too long before the capture in case they drew attention to themselves, but now they needed to move quickly to get into place. Shalom stationed the Chevrolet on Route 202, facing Garibaldi Street, and turned off the headlights. A truck was parked behind them, between their car and the railway embankment, its driver preoccupied with eating his dinner. There was nothing they could do about him now.

Aharoni stopped the Buick limousine on Garibaldi Street, ten yards in from Route 202, facing Eichmann's house. Tabor and Malkin stepped out into the cold and lifted the hood. Tabor bent over the engine; he would be hidden from Eichmann when he turned onto the street. On the limousine's front left side, Malkin leaned slightly forward as well, as though he were watching Tabor's efforts with the engine.

Eitan climbed into the backseat, his forehead pressed against the cold glass as he kept his eyes trained on the bus stop. From the driver's seat, Aharoni stared in the same direction through a pair of night-vision binoculars. There was no reason for them to speak; they only had to wait and to watch.

Seconds before bus 203 was scheduled to show, a boy wearing a bright red jacket, about fifteen years old, pedaled down Garibaldi Street on his bicycle. He stopped at the limousine. Aharoni stepped halfway out of the car — he was the only one of them who spoke any Spanish. He knew he needed to get this boy out of there, quick and quiet.

The boy asked what was wrong with their car, if they needed help. Aharoni smiled at the boy, saying, "Thank you! No need!

You can carry on your way." The boy took off, his unzipped jacket flapping around him in the wind as he disappeared into the darkness.

Then 7:40 P.M. passed, and the bus still had not shown up. Three minutes later, they saw the lights of a vehicle approaching from the direction of San Fernando. They had spent enough nights on the railway embankment to know that it was the bus.

Malkin prepared himself, repeating the words *"Un momentito, señor"* over and over in his head, gauging where in relation to the road and the car he would make his move. Tabor readied to drop the hood and help him. They would have to keep Eichmann from screaming — but they had practiced plenty. Malkin was to seize him by the throat, spin behind him, and drag him toward the open car door. Tabor would grab his legs and help throw him into the backseat. Both reminded themselves that they were not to hurt Eichmann. They had no guns, nor any need of them.

The lights from the bus cut through the night. They braced themselves. But instead of stopping opposite the kiosk, the bus kept going, past the second capture car and underneath the railway embankment. Then it was gone. It had not even slowed down near its usual stop.

A rush of doubt overcame the team. Had Eichmann altered his schedule or gone on vacation? Had he returned early from work? Worst of all, had he learned of their presence and fled from Buenos Aires?

Malkin looked toward the Eichmanns' house. Only a single lamp was lit. Typically, after their target returned home from work, there was a lot more light and activity. He was definitely not at home, but this did not rule out the possibility that he had taken the week off, or disappeared completely. After all, because of the rush to switch safe houses and to finalize their plans, the team had not watched Garibaldi Street for two nights.

The surge of expectation slowly ebbed. Nobody wanted to voice the concern they all shared: They might have missed their opportunity.

The wind continued to strengthen. Thunder from the approaching storm grew closer, and now and then there was a burst of lightning in the distance. Every few minutes, a train roared by on the tracks.

Five minutes passed. Then ten. Another bus came down the highway. The team readied for action again, but this bus did not stop either. The possibility that Eichmann had simply missed his usual bus was becoming unlikely.

Shalom and Gat got out of the Chevrolet and stood on Route 202, looking over at the limousine to see if there was any movement. According to their plan, if Eichmann did not show up by eight o'clock, they would leave and come back the next day. The longer they stayed in the target area, the greater the chance the police would happen upon them.

Behind them, they heard the sudden start of an engine. They whirled to see the truck that had been parked to their rear take off down the highway. At least that driver was no longer a concern.

After taking a few steps closer to Garibaldi Street and seeing no activity at the limousine, Shalom decided to wait. He did not want to go over to talk to Eitan, because if somebody was watching them, they could then connect the two cars. He would stay where he was until he saw the limousine pull away.

As 8 P.M., their deadline to leave, arrived, Aharoni turned in his seat and asked Eitan, "Do we take off or wait?"

Eitan had made up his mind when the first bus had passed without stopping. He knew they were jeopardizing their chances to come back the next day, but he also knew that the team was more ready now than it would ever be again. "No, we stay," he said firmly.

The minutes passed slowly: 8:01, 8:02. They all stared down Route 202. Tabor and Malkin felt certain that Eichmann was not coming, that they would have to spend more nights mentally preparing for the moment when they would grab him. They waited for the word from Eitan to close the hood and pack up.

At 8:05 P.M., headlights broke the darkness once again.

• • •

Isser Harel sat alone in a café not far from Tira, sipping a hot tea with brandy. He had checked out of the Claridge Hotel that morning and left his suitcase in a railway-station locker. If the operation met with disaster or if he were followed, he could disappear without a trace. Which was all well and good, except that he was so miserable with fever that even thinking of attempting such an escape felt beyond him at that moment.

He checked his watch: almost eight o'clock. His men would already have Eichmann in their hands — if everything had gone as planned. He did not expect anyone to come to the café to inform him of their success or otherwise for at least another forty-five minutes.

He kept his mind off what might have gone wrong by mulling over what he expected Vera Eichmann to do when her husband did not come home. There was no way she could go straight to the police, Harel was sure. She would only be reporting a missing husband — a common enough occurrence that the Argentine police would not marshal their forces to investigate. Only if she confessed that Ricardo Klement was Adolf Eichmann would a serious search be launched. Before she took that step, she and her sons would no doubt check the local hospitals and Eichmann's workplace, which would give Harel's team at least a couple of days' lead time — maybe more. Then again, they could not rule out a hunt by Eichmann's sons or by his Nazi associates and their friends in the German community . . .

These theories were just that — theories — until Harel knew the result of the operation. He stared at the hands on his watch, growing more and more anxious with every passing minute to learn what was happening on Garibaldi Street.

● ● ●

Bus 203 pulled up to the kiosk. As it came to a halt, Shalom returned to the wheel of the Chevrolet, ready to start the engine and turn on the headlights. Gat was beside him in the passenger's seat. At the limousine, Tabor repositioned himself over the engine, hidden from sight. Aharoni raised his binoculars again, and Malkin and Eitan looked toward the bus stop.

Two people got off the bus. The first was the stout woman who usually arrived with Eichmann at 7:40 P.M. She stepped down and turned left, away from Garibaldi Street. The second passenger was a man, but it was impossible to identify him in the dark.

The bus pulled away, moving past the Chevrolet down Route 202.

The man walked toward Garibaldi Street.

"Someone's coming," Aharoni whispered to Eitan, "but I can't see who it is."

Eitan looked into the darkness, but his vision was not what it had been in the past. He saw nothing.

Shalom flicked on his headlights, and they all knew at once that the figure cast in silhouette was Eichmann. The way he walked — bent forward, a determined gait — was unmistakable.

"It's him," Aharoni declared.

The two words electrified Eitan. He made sure Malkin and Tabor were in position, then he prepared to rush from the car should he be needed.

As Eichmann approached the Garibaldi intersection, Aharoni saw him dip his hand into the right pocket of his trench coat.

"He may have a gun," Aharoni said. "Should I warn Peter?"

"Yes, tell him to watch the hand," Eitan replied.

Malkin was counting out in his head exactly how many steps away Eichmann was, wanting to meet him a few feet from the tail end of the limousine. Lightning coursed through the sky. A roll of thunder followed as Malkin edged forward. He was certain that if Eichmann made a run for it across the field, he could catch him long before the older man reached his house.

Twenty yards away now. Malkin passed the driver's door. Aharoni held out his hand. "Peter, he has a hand in his pocket. Watch out for a gun."

The warning unnerved Malkin. Nobody should be saying anything to him at this moment, he thought. He did not want to be hearing about a gun. His every move had been practiced without a weapon in the equation. This changed everything.

Eichmann turned the corner. Fifteen yards away now. Malkin saw how the man was leaning into the wind, collar upturned, his right hand deep in his pocket.

Aharoni turned on the limousine's engine. Eichmann looked in their direction, but he maintained his stride.

Malkin kept moving forward. If a gun was involved, he would have to adjust how he grabbed Eichmann. He had to make sure that Eichmann never freed the weapon — if he had one — from his pocket.

Five yards. Malkin stepped into his path, and Eichmann drew up to a stop.

"*Un momentito, señor*," Malkin said, the words coming out uneasily. He locked his gaze with Eichmann's and saw the Nazi's eyes widen in fear. Eichmann stepped back. He was about to run.

Malkin burst forward, one hand reaching out to keep Eichmann's right arm down in case he had a gun. His momentum, mixed with his target's retreat, sent them both pitching to the ground. The agent seized Eichmann as they rolled into the shallow, muddy ditch that ran alongside the road. Landing on his back, Malkin tried to keep hold of Eichmann's right arm and at the same time grab his throat to cut off any call for help. Eichmann kicked, elbowed, and clawed to free himself, loosening the grip on his throat.

Then he screamed. Aharoni revved the engine to drown out the wail. Tabor hurried over to the ditch to help Malkin. Eitan also leapt from the car. Eichmann shrieked and shrieked. His house was roughly thirty yards away, close enough for anyone outside to hear his cries — or anyone inside if the windows were open. They had to silence him immediately and get out of there.

When Tabor reached the ditch, Eichmann was pressing his feet against its side to gain some leverage against Malkin, who had his arms locked around his waist. The more Eichmann fought, the more fiercely Malkin tightened his grasp. There was no way the Nazi was going to get loose. Tabor grabbed Eichmann's legs, further canceling any chance of resistance. Eichmann went slack and abruptly stopped screaming. Malkin rose to his feet, and he and Tabor hauled their captive out of the ditch and over to the limousine.

On Route 202, Shalom waited with Gat and the doctor, desperate to know what was happening. They had lost sight of Eichmann the moment he turned onto Garibaldi Street. Then they heard shouting, followed by silence. Seconds ticked by as if they were hours. Their instructions were to move only after the limousine did.

Eitan helped Malkin and Tabor get Eichmann into the backseat. Tabor hurried around the front of the limousine to close the hood, while Malkin kept his gloved hand over the captive's mouth. Eitan blindfolded him, using motorbike goggles whose lenses were covered with black tape. The second that Tabor slid into the passenger's seat, Aharoni gunned the limousine and pulled away. Only twenty-five seconds had passed since Malkin first reached for Eichmann.

Aharoni swung left at the end of the street. A hundred yards from the Eichmann house, he looked over his shoulder and ordered their captive in German, "Sit still and nothing will happen to you. If you resist, we will shoot you. Do you understand?"

Malkin took his hand away from Eichmann's mouth, but Eichmann said nothing.

"If you resist, we will shoot you. Do you understand?"

Again, no response. They thought he might have passed out.

Aharoni headed eastward, even though Tira was located to the southwest of the city. That way, if anybody saw the cars leave the area, they would point the police in the wrong direction. Malkin and Tabor bound Eichmann's hands and feet, pushed him onto the floor, and covered him with a heavy wool blanket. They searched his trench coat, but he had no gun, just a flashlight.

Eitan looked in the sideview mirror for their backup car. It was nowhere to be seen.

"Where are they?" Malkin asked.

A moment later, headlights appeared. Shalom steered the Chevrolet alongside the limousine just long enough to receive a thumbs-up. The relief on his face was clear as he sped ahead of them, now acting as the lead car.

As Aharoni settled back behind the Chevrolet, he spoke to their captive again, this time in Spanish. "What language do you speak?"

The prisoner remained quiet, breathing heavily. A few minutes later, he leaned up slightly and said in flawless German, "I am already resigned to my fate."

It was not what they expected to hear, but the words reassured the Mossad agents. Their captive spoke native German, and clearly knew why he was being kidnapped. It was as close to an admission that he was Adolf Eichmann as they could have hoped.

Eitan turned around and shook Malkin by the hand, congratulating him. Malkin rested back in his seat, mostly relieved. Though there was more of a struggle than he had hoped, they

False license plate used on one of the capture cars.

had their man and he was unharmed. Now they just had to return to the safe house.

A mile from Garibaldi Street, Shalom steered onto a dirt side road and stopped by a copse of trees. Aharoni followed in the limousine. Tabor and Gat hurried out of their cars and switched the Argentine license plates for blue diplomatic ones. They all had forged Austrian diplomatic papers in case they were stopped by the police or at a checkpoint, but the plates would limit the chances of that happening.

Soon they were back on the road, traveling the route that Shalom had charted after two weeks of reconnaissance. They kept to the speed limit and made sure to obey the traffic laws down to the mile-per-hour.

On the floor of the limousine, Eichmann remained still, silent.

Halfway to the safe house, they slowed at one of the two railway crossings on the route. The red lights were flashing, and the barriers lowered. They were stuck with at least a ten-minute wait. A line of cars backed up behind them. Once again, Aharoni warned Eichmann that if he uttered a word, he would be shot. He didn't move under the blanket, his breathing settled.

The four Israelis in the limousine tried to look casual — difficult, given the circumstances. Other drivers paced up and down outside their cars and smoked cigarettes while they waited for the train. Music blared through their open car doors. The storm that had threatened a downpour earlier passed overhead without breaking.

Finally, what seemed like hours later, the train roared by and the barriers lifted. The line of traffic eased forward. Shalom drove away, with the limousine close behind. Ten minutes from Tira, Shalom took a wrong turn, but Aharoni stayed on the proper route. Shalom spun the car around and soon caught up. Five minutes away, they parked for a second on a side road to change the diplomatic plates for a new set of Argentine ones.

At 8:55 P.M., the two cars slowed in front of Tira. A waiting Medad pulled open the gate. Aharoni rolled the limousine into the garage, and Medad closed the door behind him. After fifteen years on the run, Adolf Eichmann was now a prisoner of the Jewish people.

CHAPTER 12

Eichmann staggered uneasily into the safe house, his arms held tightly by Shalom and Malkin. The entire team accompanied him through the kitchen and upstairs to his prepared cell. Everybody stayed quiet. Harel had made it clear he wanted only Aharoni to speak to the prisoner. They all crammed into the small bedroom, which held a bed, two wooden chairs, and a table. A lightbulb blazed from a cord in the ceiling. Malkin and Shalom released their prisoner.

Eichmann stood in the middle of the room. His trench coat was splattered with mud from the struggle in the ditch. He was silent, his back straight as a board, arms down at his sides, his eyes still covered with the goggles. Only his hands moved, clenching and unclenching nervously.

Aharoni brought Eichmann over to the bed, and the team stripped his clothes off him. He never protested, looking helpless in his frayed, grubby underwear and socks. Aharoni could not fathom how this sad, pathetic creature could be Adolf Eichmann, once the master of the lives of millions of Jews.

Dr. Elian inspected Eichmann's body and mouth for any hidden cyanide capsules, which might be used to commit suicide in the event of capture. He removed the prisoner's false teeth and examined those as well.

Eichmann broke the silence, his voice strained but clear: "No man can be vigilant for fifteen years."

The team used this list of identifying marks to confirm Eichmann's identity.

Next, Elian checked Eichmann's vital signs — his temperature, pulse, breathing rate, and blood pressure — to make sure he was not on the verge of collapse. Then, at the direction of Aharoni, he examined him for any distinguishing marks, as listed in the Mossad's file on Eichmann. He found several scars that matched medical certificates and witness testimonies, including an inch-and-a-half-long pale scar below his left eyebrow and one above his left elbow. Malkin and Shalom dressed the prisoner in loose pajamas, laid him flat on the bed, and handcuffed his left ankle to the bed frame. They left his goggles on to further his disorientation. This was the moment when Eichmann was most vulnerable.

Aharoni was eager to take advantage of his subject's unbalanced state and begin his interrogation. While he lacked experience as an undercover operative, as an interrogator Aharoni was unequaled in the Shin Bet. He never used force, knowing that physical abuse only led to false confessions. Instead, he wore his subjects down with staccato bursts of questions, twisting them in their own lies and hammering them with known facts until the truth was the only way out. He was prepared for a long night.

At 9:15 P.M., the room empty but for Aharoni and Shalom, the interrogation began. Aharoni had Eichmann's entire file memorized, so there would be no delay in asking follow-up questions.

"What's your name?" he asked sharply.

"Ricardo Klement," the prisoner said.

"What was your previous name?"

"Otto Heninger."

Aharoni took a long, tense breath. He had never heard the name, and the manner in which his subject was answering his questions, coolly and credibly, put him off. He switched tactics.

"When was your third son born?"

"On March 29, 1942."

"What is his name?"

"Dieter."

"How tall are you?"

"Five feet, eight inches."

"What is your size in shoes?" Aharoni asked. The faster he asked the questions, the less time his subject would have to waver or decide to start lying.

"Nine."

"What size in shirt?"

"Forty-four."

Eichmann responded as quickly as the questions came, and his answers lined up with what Aharoni had read in the file. The prisoner was telling the truth.

"What was the number of your membership card in the National Socialist Party?" he asked.

"889895," the man said, definitely and without pause. This was Eichmann's number. It was a critical admission.

"What was your number in the SS?"

"45326."

Klement was Eichmann. Aharoni was sure. Now he needed Eichmann to admit it, to come clean. The interrogator looked across the bed at Shalom. They were both eager for their prisoner to confess his true identity, and they knew they were close.

"When did you come to Argentina?"

"1950."

"What is your name?"

"Ricardo Klement."

He was still resisting, but his hands were trembling slightly. He must have known that he had revealed himself with his identification numbers.

"Was your SS number 45326?"

"Yes."

"What is your date of birth?"

"March 19, 1906."

"Where were you born?"

"Solingen."

Aharoni had him. He knew it. Shalom knew it. Their prisoner knew it. The interrogator asked one last question.

"Under what name were you born?"

"Adolf Eichmann."

Joy erupted in the room. Aharoni and Shalom shook hands over the prisoner. They had their man.

Eichmann spoke again, this time in an ingratiating tone. "You can quite easily understand that I'm agitated. I would like to ask for a little wine, if it's possible — red wine — to help me control my emotions."

Aharoni replied that they would bring him something to drink.

"As soon as you told me to keep quiet, there in the car, I knew I was in the hands of Israelis," Eichmann continued. "I know Hebrew. I learned it from Rabbi Leo Baeck. *Sh'ma Yisrael, Ha'Shem Elokeinu —*"

"That's enough," Aharoni said sharply. The words were the beginning of the Sh'ma, the holiest prayer in the Jewish religion, recited in the morning and at night by the faithful. It was the prayer spoken at the hour of death, and millions, *millions*, of Jews had come to utter it because of Adolf Eichmann. Disgusted, the agents left the room to regain control over their emotions and fight the temptation to beat up their prisoner.

Once they had calmed down, Aharoni returned to his questioning. For another hour, he asked about Eichmann's family: the birth dates and birthplaces of his sons and brothers, of his wife, of his extended family. They already knew they had their man, but they wanted to be absolutely sure.

Finally, Eitan ended the interrogation. Aharoni and Shalom left to report to Isser Harel. They drove into Buenos Aires and dropped the Buick limousine off in a parking lot, not daring to use it again. When they reached the café, it was a few minutes shy of midnight. Harel was paying his check, ready to move on to the next rendezvous location on his list. When he saw Shalom and Aharoni, disheveled and tired though they looked, he knew that they had succeeded. As Shalom gave his report, Harel's mind was already focused on what would come next: getting Eichmann to Israel.

They left the café soon after and went off in separate directions. Harel hurried to a nearby restaurant, where a sayan, recruited by Ilani, was expecting him. Harel recognized "Meir Lavi" by the placement of a certain book on his table. Lavi had been moving from café to café for as many hours as Harel had, not knowing the purpose of his actions nor who he was supposed to meet.

Harel cut straight to the chase. He told Lavi to go to Ilani at the embassy and say, "The typewriter is okay."

"That's all?" Lavi asked, upset he had spent half the night waiting to pass along a message that seemed like gibberish.

The question was met with a stern glance from Harel.

"I'll go to him at once," Lavi said.

The message translated to Eichmann being in Israeli hands. Harel knew it would be passed on to Mossad headquarters, then to David Ben-Gurion and his Foreign Minister, Golda Meir. He walked to the railway station to collect his bag. With each step through the brisk night in Buenos Aires, he slowly realized the significance of what they had done. For this moment only, he allowed himself to enjoy their success.

Back on Garibaldi Street, Vera Eichmann waited anxiously for her husband to come home. She had expected him to be late, but not this late. Something was wrong. Vera had always feared that her husband's enemies would finally catch up with him. She decided to tell her sons that their father had not come home. They would find him, she knew.

Near midnight, Peter Malkin knocked on Rafi Eitan's open door in Tira. "I'm going back," he said. He had noticed that Eichmann's glasses were missing, and a search of the limousine had not turned them up. If the glasses were discovered on Garibaldi Street, Vera Eichmann would have immediate proof that her husband had been abducted.

He drove alone into San Fernando, then caught a late-night bus to the kiosk. A cold, wet wind blew across the plain as he walked toward the capture site. The same single kerosene lamp he had seen earlier burned in the Eichmann house. They were still expecting him.

Malkin searched the road and the ditch with a small flashlight and found some broken glass in the mud by the side of the road — but not the frames. He continued to look in the scrub beyond the ditch, but without success. He knew he had better get out of there; someone might see him if he stayed too long.

Hours later, Malkin pulled back into the driveway of the safe house. As he was making his way to the door, something suddenly jumped on his back. Malkin spun and grabbed a fistful of fur. A white cat. He released the screeching animal, cursing not only it but also himself for being so on edge.

The house was quiet and cold. Like a tomb, its thick masonry walls deadened any sound and kept a chill in the air. Five of the operatives were staying at Tira: Eitan, Malkin, Medad, Gat, and Tabor. This was only the first night, one of nine to come — maybe more — before Eichmann could be flown out. It was plenty of time for the police, the Argentine security services, or Eichmann's sons and associates to find them. The Mossad team had to wait and hope that their precautions would keep them safe.

Their contingency plans provided for the police storming the house. But what if they were discovered by a group of Nazi sympathizers? They might find themselves fending off an assault, or a siege. Tabor had already resolved that if this were to happen, he would take Eichmann into the crawl space above his cell and strangle him.

Eitan had instituted a twenty-four-hour watch in rotating three-hour shifts. A guard was stationed in Eichmann's room at all times, the door always open, the light always on, and Eitan slept in the adjoining room so that he would always be nearby. He wanted the goggles to stay on the prisoner until they had him safely in Israel. This would not only hamper Eichmann's chances of escape, but if he did somehow manage to get away, he would be unable to identify anybody on the Mossad team.

Throughout the night, Eichmann remained restless. He refused to eat anything and did not sleep. He lay on the bed, flat on his back, his face clenching and relaxing seemingly beyond his control. Sometimes he tried to adjust his position, clanking the handcuffs attached to his thin ankle against the iron bed frame.

After daybreak, Yaakov Gat lifted up Eichmann in bed, gave him a glass of orange juice, and spoon-fed him some eggs and crackers. The prisoner ate, but his hands shook constantly.

Zvi Aharoni arrived soon after breakfast and took up his interrogation where he had left off.

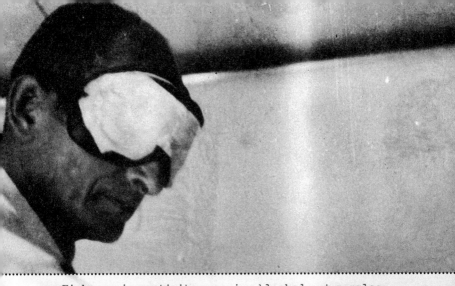

Eichmann in captivity, wearing blacked-out goggles.

"I just have a few simple questions for you," he said. "Answer them, and we won't have any problems."

"Yes, sir," Eichmann answered obediently. The two men sat at arm's length from each other in the small room.

"Why did you use the name 'Otto Heninger' last night?"

"That was my name for more than four years."

"Where was that?"

"In Germany. I worked there as a lumberjack before coming to Argentina."

"Why didn't your family live under the name Klement, like you?" Aharoni asked.

It was an obvious question. If Eichmann had only insisted that his sons take his alias surname, then Sylvia Hermann would never have been able to make the connection between Nick and his Nazi father.

"You don't expect me to ask my family to lie for me," Eichmann said.

Aharoni was disgusted. Eichmann had made his family lie for him for years. The answer was typical of many he would receive, as Eichmann perceived a twisted reality that matched his own ego.

Under the prior instructions of Isser Harel, Aharoni questioned Eichmann about other former Nazis living in Argentina. Eichmann suggested that they would be too worried about saving their own skins to do much about finding him. It was clear to Aharoni that Eichmann thought little of his former colleagues.

On the interrogation continued, hour after hour. Eichmann remained calm and forthcoming, at least about his own life. Aharoni felt he had built enough trust with the prisoner to ask a key question.

"Are you prepared to come and stand trial in Israel?" he said.

Haim Cohen had advised Aharoni that it would be better if Eichmann came willingly to Israel. The Attorney General wanted, if possible, a signed statement to that effect.

"No. Definitely not," Eichmann said. He spoke forcefully, as if he had been waiting for the question. "Number one: I did nothing wrong. All I did was follow orders. You could never prove that I committed a crime. Number two: What . . . what do I have to do with Israel? I'm a German. You can put me . . . If, at all, if I did commit any crime, I should be judged in Germany. Or in Argentina, I am a citizen here. But not in Israel."

"You know that nobody will put you on trial except the Israelis," Aharoni said. "It's Israel or nowhere. Don't worry. It won't be a kangaroo trial. It will be a proper trial. You will have a lawyer."

Eichmann hesitated, then said, "I will think about it."

CHAPTER 13

On May 12, Nick Eichmann was putting in an elevator control box at an apartment building in Buenos Aires when his younger brother Dieter rushed toward him. Short of breath, Dieter said, "The old man is gone!"

The screwdriver in Nick's hand fell to the floor. In a rush of words, Dieter explained their father had not come home the night before. The brothers immediately agreed that he must have been assaulted, probably by Jews — maybe even by Israelis.

They went to see one of the leading figures in the expatriate German community, Carlos Fuldner, the man who had helped their father get into Argentina. They feared that whoever had taken their father might also want to abduct their mother and youngest brother. Their other brother, Horst, was away with the merchant navy, so it was down to the two of them.

Fuldner calmed Dieter and Nick, explaining coolly, reasonably, that there were three plausible reasons why their father failed to come home. First, the police might have arrested him for drunkenness or some other infraction and kept him overnight in jail. Second, he might have been involved in an accident and taken to the hospital — or even to the mortuary. Third, his pursuers might have caught up with him, as his sons suspected, and, whether they were vigilantes or state-sponsored, they could have kidnapped or even killed him. Fuldner said they would launch a search immediately, starting with the hospitals and police stations around San Fernando. The area around the house would also be examined for any clues or signs of a struggle.

Inquiries at the San Fernando police station and nearby hospitals came up with nothing. Vera Eichmann went to Mercedes-Benz, where she learned that Ricardo Klement had worked the previous day and then stayed late for a union meeting. He had not shown up for work that morning.

Then a search around Garibaldi Street turned up Eichmann's broken glasses in the ditch, pressed into the mud. There was no doubt now: He had been taken.

Nick and Dieter pawned some gold rings and watches for three guns — a .22-caliber pistol, a .38, and a .45. Despite Fuldner's assurances, they very quickly realized that the German community would not help them. Most of their father's associates wanted nothing to do with them. Nor could they ask for police help without revealing their father's true identity, which might place him in even more danger. Instead, they decided to turn to their connections in a radical nationalist organization called Tacuara.

Tacuara had been founded a few years previously by a group of young, mostly upper-middle-class, high school and university students. They took their name from the makeshift weapon used by gauchos in the fight for Argentine independence — essentially a knife tied to the end of a sugarcane. Fiercely Catholic, Tacuara was militant, fascist, and anti-Semitic. Its aims included freeing Argentina from liberal democracy, capitalism, and Jewish influence. New members swore an oath of allegiance in a graveyard, wore gray shirts and armbands stitched with the Maltese cross, idolized Hitler and Mussolini, and used the Nazi salute.

Neo-Nazis rally at a theater in Buenos Aires in 1964.

They were often seen roaming the city on motorcycles. Though not in Tacuara themselves, Nick and Dieter shared similar political views and had friends who were members.

The idea of a group of Jews, possibly Israelis, operating illegally inside Argentina inflamed Tacuara, and some of its members rallied to hunt them down.

●●●

Peter Malkin was on guard when Eichmann turned to him, still wearing the blacked-out goggles. "Are you the man who captured me?" Eichmann said.

"Yes, my name is Maxim," Malkin answered hesitatingly, giving his alias.

Rafi Eitan had given direct orders not to speak to the prisoner, but Malkin wanted to know why Eichmann had managed the slaughter of the Jewish people and how he had been capable of doing so. With Eichmann speaking in German and Malkin in Yiddish, the conversation was rough and stumbling.

Malkin remembered when he had watched Eichmann playing with his young son outside his home. "Your boy, he reminds me so much of my sister's son," Malkin said.

"What happened to him?"

"Nothing happened," Malkin answered bitterly. But then he continued, "There is only one thing I know: Your boy is alive, and the boy of my sister is dead."

"Are you going to kill me?" Eichmann asked.

"No. We're going to bring you to trial, to a fair trial — a chance you never gave your victims."

Then Malkin asked Eichmann, "How did you come to do what you did?"

"It was an order. I had a job to do."

"Just a job?" Malkin said.

"Are you not a soldier? Don't you have your orders? You captured me. Why did you do it? Because of an order."

"Yes, I got an order to capture you, but there's a big difference between you and me. I had an order to catch a criminal. But you went after innocent people. They had done nothing wrong at all. You followed those orders because you hated these people."

"No . . . I, in a way, I love Jews."

Malkin could hardly believe what he was hearing. "You love Jews? Then what were you doing in the SS?"

"I wanted them to have their own country. I wanted to send them away. We didn't want to do anything to the Jews. At first, we just talked about cleaning the Jews from Germany. But there was no nation that would accept them. We talked about Madagascar and all kinds of other plans. I even went to Palestine in 1936."

It sounded to Malkin like Eichmann was already preparing his defense. As they talked over the course of many of the nights that followed, he was sickened by Eichmann's denials and by his inability to view his actions against the Jews through anything other than the Nazi mind-set — even after fifteen years.

The agents had mentally prepared themselves for the risks of holing up at the house — possibly even having to face an assault from the police or from Eichmann's sons and associates if they were located. But not one of them had anticipated the soul-hollowing effect of inhabiting the same space as Adolf Eichmann.

They had to feed him, dress him, shave him, and bring him to the toilet. Too scared to attempt any resistance, Eichmann was obedient to the point of subservience. He asked permission before having a bowel movement, and when he was finished he asked for some toilet paper. This was the man who had sent many of their own families to their deaths. It would have been easier had they felt only hatred toward him, but he seemed barely worthy of the emotion.

● ● ●

At Ezeiza Airport, Yosef Klein had secured all the clearances and permissions for the El Al flight. He was now finalizing the fuel, catering, and cleaning services. He continued to charm the airport staff, who now allowed him to walk unchallenged through security and around the airport. He had also introduced them to Avraham Shalom, who was posing as a diplomatic official, and the recently arrived El Al security chief, Adi Peleg. Together, the three men reconnoitered the airport for the most discreet way to get Eichmann onto the plane.

The day after Eichmann's capture, Klein joined Harel at one of his cafés. Using Klein's information, they came up with three possibilities for bringing the prisoner on board. The first was putting him in a crate stamped as diplomatic cargo; the second, hiding him in a caterer's cart to be forklifted on board before departure; the third, dressing him in an El Al uniform and passing him through inspection with the crew.

All three plans had their strengths and weaknesses.

Shalom had no intention of leaving this part of the operation in the hands of a civilian, even one as competent as Klein. He tried to pass through security every few hours so that the guards got used to seeing him. He determined that the guards watching the side entrance to the maintenance area would be the easiest to deceive. They were more concerned about theft than any other kind of security breach.

If Eichmann were dressed in an El Al uniform, perhaps sedated by the doctor, Shalom thought they should be able to get him past these guards without difficulty. Smuggling him on board in a caterer's cart or a diplomatic crate would be too complicated. Shalom liked simple and straightforward.

Next was the question of how soon the plane could take off after Eichmann was on board, who would give permission for it to leave, and what to do if there was a delay. Shalom thoroughly interrogated Klein and Peleg about every eventuality. The escape from Argentina had to be planned as meticulously as the capture itself.

● ● ●

On May 15, sensing he was making strides in his interrogation of Eichmann, Aharoni again asked him to sign a statement declaring he would go of his own accord to Israel and stand trial. Aharoni had already written a draft text for him to copy. To his frustration, Eichmann refused, at one point suggesting that he might go to Austria instead.

"Stop insulting me!" Aharoni snapped. "It will be either Israel or nowhere at all. Either you agree or you refuse. But do not cloud the issue. If you have committed no wrong, then you have nothing to fear. Think about it. We have lots of time."

That night, Harel visited Tira to see Eichmann and congratulate his agents on the successful capture. When he had met with Rafi Eitan earlier, Harel had been shocked by his low spirits. Now he found the rest of the team equally depressed. Harel had always suspected that it would be stressful to guard Eichmann, but he did not understand the debilitating effect until he went upstairs to see the prisoner himself.

Eichmann was lying on the bed in his pajamas, the goggles over his eyes. Harel was stunned at how ordinary and pathetic he looked. He later wrote about his agents' mood: "The sight of that miserable runt, who had lost every vestige of his former superiority and arrogance the moment he was stripped of his uniform and powers of authority, gave them a feeling of insult and profound scorn. Was this the personification of evil? Was this the tool used by a diabolic government? This nonentity, devoid of human dignity and pride, was this the messenger of death for six million Jews?"

Harel suggested Eitan give each agent a day's leave, one at a time. While pulling on his overcoat, he rallied his team: "I know what you've all been through. All you have to do is hang on for a couple of days." In truth, Harel feared that if something went wrong with the El Al plane, his team might be waiting for much longer than a couple of days.

By May 17, the mood at the safe house had darkened, and the boredom was oppressive. Downstairs, they listened intently to the radio for mention of Klement or Eichmann — anything that might indicate his capture had gained the notice of the police.

There was not much else they could do when not on guard duty. The house had a few books in English, but those who could read that language had long since exhausted the supply. They played chess, stared out the windows at the neighbors going about their lives, and even invented games, such as an apple-eating contest. Malkin spent time sketching pictures of Eichmann and also of his own family, from memory, including his sister, Fruma.

A few tasks did offer some relief from the strain of idleness. Tabor built a large wooden crate with four leather straps inside to secure the prisoner's arms and legs. He drilled fifty breathing holes into the wood and labeled the crate as diplomatic post: FROM: ISRAELI EMBASSY, BUENOS AIRES. TO: FOREIGN MINISTRY, JERUSALEM. He also constructed a concealed chamber in an airplane catering cart that Yosef Klein had smuggled out of the airport. Shalom planned to bring Eichmann on board as part of the El Al crew, but there was always the chance that they might need a backup plan.

An Israeli passport, a visa, a driver's license, health certifications, and an El Al badge were required to pass Eichmann off as "crewmate Zeev Zichroni." Shalom Dani came to the safe house to prepare the documents. When he entered the cell to take new photographs of Eichmann, the color drained from his face and his hands began to tremble. Eichmann had been given a close

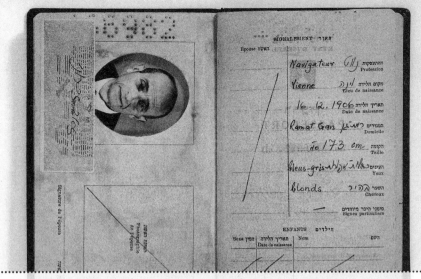

The fake passport for "Zeev Zichroni," created by Shalom Dani.

shave and dressed in a suit. Makeup had been applied to his face, and he looked startlingly younger and more imposing — more like his wartime photograph.

Dani said nothing to Eichmann other than to direct him how to pose for the photographs. The minute they were complete, he left the room. He had intended to confront Eichmann, to tell him what he had done to his family, but he had not expected such a rush of emotions. "To even be in the same room with him, I had to force myself not to feel anything," he told the others before withdrawing into another room to work on his forgeries. When he emerged, he handed Eitan the documents and left Tira without saying good-bye. He had only one thing on his mind: getting some fresh air.

CHAPTER 14

On a clear, bright Tel Aviv afternoon, May 18, 1960, the delegation for the Argentine anniversary celebrations boarded their Bristol Britannia 4X-AGD at Lod Airport. Cameras snapped as the delegates climbed the mobile staircase to the long, sleek plane with the Israeli flag painted on its tail. At the top of the steps, Abba Eban, the head of the delegation, smiled for the cameras and waved good-bye to the dignitaries who had come to see them off. Though a member of Ben-Gurion's cabinet, Eban was a "minister without portfolio," which made him ideal for a diplomatic mission to Argentina.

Ben-Gurion had personally informed Eban several days before that the flight was being sent to Argentina to collect Eichmann. None of the others had the slightest idea of the flight's special purpose. All of the delegation members, including Eban, were scheduled to return to Israel on American civilian airlines — ostensibly because the Britannia was needed back earlier for its regular routes.

Every effort at secrecy could not keep the crew members from suspecting that there might be more to this flight than the airline had told them. First, there were three men in El Al uniforms whom none of the crew had ever seen before. Second, a number of the El Al employees were used to participating in "monkey business crews," which assisted the Shin Bet or Mossad on operations. When enough of these special crew members were brought together for a flight, it usually meant there was a hidden agenda.

After checking the crew roster, Captain Shmuel Wedeles, one of two copilots selected by Tohar for the mission, was sure there was an ulterior motive. A Viennese Jew who, as a child, had seen a mob force an elderly rabbi to eat forbidden pork before setting his beard on fire, Wedeles had escaped alone to Israel; the rest of his family had died in the Holocaust. He had been a member of the Haganah, the paramilitary organization that preceded the Israeli defense forces, and a pilot in the War of Independence. As soon as he saw Yehuda Shimoni on the plane, he asked him bluntly, "Who are they bringing, Mengele or Eichmann?" Josef Mengele was a doctor who performed horrific medical experiments on children in Auschwitz, and he had long been rumored to live in South America. Shimoni denied the implication, but his look of astonishment told Wedeles everything he needed to know.

The Bristol Britannia 4X-AGD used by El Al for the mission.

The chief purser was also suspicious. When he asked his friend Tohar what was going on, the pilot cryptically said, "You won't be sorry you've been chosen to participate in the flight."

Once all the passengers had settled into their places and the crew was ready, loudspeakers in the terminal building and outside on the tarmac boomed in Hebrew and then in English, "Announcing the departure of Flight 601, Tel Aviv to Buenos Aires." The four turbo-propelled engines hummed to life, and the airplane taxied toward the runway. At exactly 1:05 P.M., the wheels lifted off Israeli soil, and the journey to Argentina began. The plane would stop to refuel in Rome, Italy; Dakar, Senegal; and Recife, Brazil, before flying seven and a half hours south to Buenos Aires. They were scheduled to arrive in Argentina on the afternoon of May 19.

• • •

That night, Nick and Dieter Eichmann broke into a Jewish synagogue in the city, guns at their sides. A former SS officer they knew through their father had tipped them off that he might be in the basement. A search revealed nothing: The synagogue was empty.

Throughout Buenos Aires, Tacuara members were patrolling on their motorcycles, watching the airport as well as the bus and train stations. They also staked out synagogues and checked the hospitals and morgues in every neighborhood. A heavy police presence for the anniversary celebrations did little to slow their search.

Nick and Dieter had no idea whether their father was still alive. For all they knew, he might have already been shot, his body buried. His assailants might well be long gone by now. With each passing day, the two brothers grew more and more desperate.

Some of the young firebrands who were assisting them urged Dieter and Nick to make a bold move if they wanted to have any chance of finding their father. They had no doubt the Israelis were behind the abduction, and they suggested kidnapping the Israeli Ambassador, offering him in trade. If the Israelis refused to negotiate, they could torture their captive until Eichmann was returned. But a former SS officer helping them warned, "Don't do anything stupid. Stay reasonable. Or you will lose everything — absolutely everything." They dropped the kidnapping idea and continued with their search.

●●●

"Let me ask you this," Peter Malkin said to Eichmann in the early morning hours of May 19. "When it was determined that the policy was not to be resettlement but death, how did you feel about that?"

"There was nothing to be done. The order came from the Führer himself."

"But how did you feel?"

"There was nothing to be done."

"I see. So you turned into a killer."

"No, that's not true. I never killed anyone," Eichmann said. "I was involved in collection and transport."

Malkin did not understand how Eichmann could convince himself that he had done nothing wrong.

Eichmann went on to explain how diligent he had been in making his schedules. Malkin interjected, "You do realize we are

Eichmann's Long Arm, a drawing by Peter Malkin, completed during the time Eichmann was in captivity in Buenos Aires.

talking about innocent people here? Small children? Old men and women?"

Eichmann showed no emotion, and Malkin understood then that the Nazi did not regret his actions against the Jews.

Twelve hours later, when it was Malkin's watch again, they picked up where they had left off. Eichmann had spoken of his love for red wine, and Malkin thought that it wouldn't do any harm to give him a glass. The prisoner had been bound to the bed for eight nights straight. Malkin brought in a bottle of wine and a record player that belonged to Yaakov Medad. Malkin poured a glass of wine and placed it in Eichmann's hands.

The prisoner drained his glass. Malkin sipped at his wine. He put a record on the turntable and then lit a cigarette for Eichmann. Flamenco music filled the small, stuffy room. Eichmann drew deeply on the cigarette until it was almost at its butt.

"Don't burn your fingers," Malkin warned.

"Why are you doing this for me?" Eichmann asked, more at ease than any time since his arrival at the house.

"I don't know," Malkin said. "I felt it was something I wanted to do for you."

Eichmann nodded, silent.

Malkin remembered the statement that Aharoni had been trying to get Eichmann to sign. This might be their opportunity.

"Eichmann, I think you are mistaken about not signing the papers to go to Jerusalem," he said.

"I don't want to go. Why can't I go to Germany?"

"I'm not going to force you to do it. If I were you, though, I would sign the papers, and I will tell you why. It's the only time in your life that you will have the opportunity to say what you think. And you will stand there in Jerusalem and tell the whole world what you think was right, in your own words."

Eichmann drained his second glass of wine. *He might be warming to the idea*, Malkin thought. Then Eichmann asked to be allowed to stand and remove his goggles. Malkin agreed. Eichmann had already seen his face the night of the capture. A second time made no difference. Still, as he helped Eichmann up and lifted the goggles from his face, the agent kept a close watch on his prisoner. This might be a trick, an attempt to escape.

At last Eichmann said, "Where is the paper?"

Malkin passed it to him, along with a pen. Eichmann read the draft, then, leaning on the night table, he copied out his statement in neat German.

I, the undersigned, Adolf Eichmann, declare of my own free will that, since my true identity has been discovered, I realize that it is futile for me to attempt to go on evading justice. I state that I am prepared to travel to Israel to stand trial in that country before a competent court. I understand that I shall receive legal aid, and I shall endeavor to give a straightforward account of the facts of my last years of service in Germany so that a true picture of the facts may be passed on to future generations. I make this declaration of my own free will. I have been promised nothing, nor have any threats been made against me. I wish at last to achieve inner peace. As I am unable to remember all the details and am confused about certain facts, I ask to be granted assistance in my endeavors to establish the truth by being given access to documents and evidence.

When he had finished, Eichmann drew back from the table. "What date should I put, yesterday's or today's?"

"Just leave it May 1960."

He signed: "Adolf Eichmann, Buenos Aires, May 1960."

"You've done a very good thing. You won't regret it," Malkin said. He gave Eichmann another cigarette. When he finished smoking it, the agent refastened the goggles over his prisoner's eyes.

Footsteps charged down the hall, and Yaakov Medad burst into the room. "What the hell are you doing?" he yelled, looking at the wine, the record player, and the cigarettes. "Throwing a party for this murderer?"

Malkin tried to explain, but Medad was furious, his face crimson. "You amuse him with my music? This butcher of my family?"

Eitan and Gat rushed to the room, fearing their prisoner might be trying to escape. Malkin tried to justify himself, showing the signed statement, but they were more worried about calming Medad then haranguing Malkin for disobeying orders. Eventually, everyone settled down, and Tabor relieved Malkin of his watch. As Malkin headed down the hall, Rafi Eitan stopped him long enough to say, "Good work."

● ● ●

Shmuel Wedeles pointed the plane down through the clouds over the South Atlantic and toward the Brazilian coast. Fifteen minutes later, they reached the radio beacon of Campina Grande, eighty nautical miles from Recife, the altimeters showing they were now at 10,000 feet. Wedeles shifted onto a southeast course toward the airport. Then he radioed air-traffic control.

"Recife Control, this is El Al 4X-AGD from Dakar to Recife, heading 135, altitude 7,500, descending, estimating Recife on the hour."

"Roger, El Al," the controller returned. "Maintain course. Report when reaching 2,000."

At an altitude of 4,000 feet, the plane had yet to descend out of the clouds. In a few minutes, they would land at the airport. Forty nautical miles away, they reached 2,000 feet. Wedeles was preparing to radio air-traffic control with their position when they finally cleared the clouds.

Straight ahead he saw an expanse of green. The plane was heading into a forest! Wedeles yanked back on the stick, bringing up the nose of the plane. At the same time, he jammed the engine throttles forward, increasing speed so as to prevent the aircraft from stalling.

The plane leveled off just above the treetops. Everyone in the flight cabin stared out the window as they flew less than a wingspan over the forest.

"My God, the Brazilians think and talk meters, not feet!" a cockpit crew member said. The Israelis measured altitude in feet, as was usual in Europe, the United States, the Middle East, and Africa, but the Brazilians measured it in meters, which were more than three times as long. When Wedeles reported that they were at 2,000 (feet), the Brazilians thought they were at the equivalent of 6,500 feet. If the cloud base had been 100 feet lower, they would have crashed straight into the trees.

Ten minutes later, at 7:05 A.M., the plane landed safely. But the Israelis' troubles were only beginning. Zvi Tohar wanted to depart from Recife as soon as they had refueled and cleaned the plane — an hour at most. To his surprise, when they taxied toward the terminal building, a red-carpet reception awaited them, including a local band and hundreds of onlookers. The airport commander, dressed in a starched uniform crowded with medals, welcomed the "overseas strangers to beautiful Brazil." Representatives of the local Jewish community celebrated their arrival. After an awkwardly staged reception, the crew and delegation left the plane to stretch their legs and grab a coffee in the terminal building.

Half an hour later, Shaul Shaul and his fellow navigator, Gady Hassin, tried to enter the control tower to file their flight plan and collect weather reports for the journey to Buenos Aires. A soldier blocked them, angrily barking, "No passage!" Hassin went to get Tohar, but the captain failed to make any headway either. The soldier was clear: "The commandant is asleep. Nobody is to disturb him."

Tohar now feared the true purpose of their flight had been exposed. He backed off from the soldier, not wanting to attract any more attention to the El Al crew.

A waiter from the terminal cafeteria approached the standoff between the soldier and crew. He was in his late twenties and, most likely, a Mossad agent stationed at the airport in case such a situation arose. He spoke briefly with the guard in fluent Portuguese, then told Tohar, "Have patience. I will go into town, and, with any luck, I'll be back within a half hour with a solution." He rode away on his bicycle.

Half an hour later, an elderly man, the secretary of the local Jewish community center, walked into the airport carrying a heavy leather bag. He came straight to the soldier and said that he needed a word with the commandant. The soldier disappeared with the bag, and the commandant himself appeared a few minutes later.

He cursed the guard before slapping him twice in the face. Then he looked at Tohar like he was an old friend. "Captain, why didn't you tell me you wanted to talk?"

With the bribe to the commandant paid, the Israelis filed their flight plan. Three hours after their scheduled departure from Recife, the Britannia moved down the runway and lifted into the sky.

At 4:05 P.M., the Britannia descended into Buenos Aires and landed on the runway with a screech. A host of diplomats from the Argentine foreign ministry were waiting to greet the plane, along with people from the Israeli embassy and the local Jewish community. The waiting band struck up the Israeli national anthem, *"Ha Tikvah"* ("The Hope"), and the children present shouted and waved tiny Israeli flags.

Shortly after the plane's arrival, Isser Harel met with Tohar and Shimoni near the airport's Hotel Internacional. Tohar now refused to land in Brazil on the return journey, saying that the Brazilians were not to be trusted. This was all right with Harel, since he wanted to fly straight from Buenos Aires to Dakar anyway to prevent the plane being seized or forced down on South American soil. They would file a false flight plan that still included Recife to throw any pursuers off their trail.

Harel then detailed the plan to bring Eichmann onto the plane disguised as an El Al crew member. He wanted the plane to depart as early as possible the following day, but Tohar insisted that the crew needed more rest, given the long flight. They were testing the Britannia's limits as it was; the added risk of an exhausted crew would be inviting disaster. Harel conceded. They would depart close to midnight on May 20.

Zvi Tohar headed to the Hotel Internacional to relay the orders to his crew. He gathered the other two pilots, Azriel Ronen and Wedeles; the navigators, Shaul and Hassin; and the flight engineers, Oved Kabiri and Shimon Blanc (a survivor of the Dachau concentration camp), together in his suite. This was the team responsible for getting the plane safely back to Israel, and Tohar felt they should know the purpose of the flight.

He told them about Eichmann and that they were going to fly nonstop from Buenos Aires to Dakar to avoid any chance of being compromised. He asked his navigators to chart a route and his flight engineers to ensure that the plane was capable of it. The crew soberly disbanded and went to try to get as much rest as they could.

CHAPTER 15

On May 20, the day of Eichmann's planned departure, the agents prepared to bring their mission to a close. Those who weren't busy with guard duty went over their new identities or worked on returning the safe houses to their original condition. Early in the afternoon, Zvi Aharoni put on a suit and tie and flagged a taxi to the Israeli embassy. There, "Yossef" provided him with a new Chevrolet limousine with diplomatic plates to take Eichmann to the airport. He also gave him a diplomatic passport, which identified Aharoni as a member of the South American desk of the Israeli Foreign Ministry, and an international driver's license.

At Maoz, Shalom Dani rushed to finish the last of Eichmann's documents. He even created an official medical certificate from a local hospital stating that "Zichroni" had suffered a head trauma in an accident but was cleared to fly. Dr. Elian had put Eichmann on a strict diet to reduce the risk of any complications from the sedatives he planned to give him.

Moshe Tabor spent most of the day at the airport. Klein had arranged for the El Al plane to be parked at the Aerolíneas Argentinas hangar, away from the main terminal. After inspecting the Britannia with the two mechanics, Tabor set about preparing a secret compartment where they could hide Eichmann if the plane was searched. He built a hinged false wall in front of one of the lavatories in the first-class cabin. When he was finished, no one would guess that there was ever a bathroom in that part of the plane.

Avraham Shalom was also at the airport, ensuring that the guards he had befriended over the past week had not been moved to different posts and that they knew he would be coming in and out of the gate throughout the day. He reconnoitered the roads from Tira one last time, finding no new checkpoints along the routes he had chosen.

Isser Harel set up his headquarters at an airport terminal restaurant. The restaurant was always crowded, the conversation and clanking dishes deafening, and people were constantly milling in and out of its doors. Harel could stay there for hours, meeting all his operatives for their briefings, without anybody giving him so much as a second glance. With the plane scheduled to depart at midnight, he knew it would be a long evening.

At 7:30 P.M., Shalom and Aharoni arrived in the smoky, cacophonous restaurant. They told Harel the team was ready for the transfer to the airport. Having received confirmation from Klein that the plane and El Al crew were also ready, Harel gave the green light.

At the safe house, the team finished the last of their preparations for departure. Those traveling with Eichmann to the airport dressed in El Al uniforms and packed their belongings. After Dr. Elian gave the prisoner a thorough physical examination, Peter Malkin dyed Eichmann's hair gray and applied makeup to his face, aging him further by drawing lines on his forehead and around his mouth, and shadowing the skin underneath his eyes. He glued a thick mustache onto Eichmann's top lip. Then he dressed him in a starched white shirt, blue pants, polished shoes, and an El Al cap with a blue Star of David on the front.

By the time Malkin finished his work, Aharoni had arrived with Yoel Goren, one of the Mossad operatives who had come on the El Al flight. Goren was the agent who, more than two years before, had investigated the house in Olivos and stated it was impossible Eichmann lived in such a shabby place. Nonetheless, he was an obvious asset in this part of the operation because of his fluent Spanish and knowledge of Buenos Aires.

Dr. Elian rolled up Eichmann's right sleeve and wiped his arm using a cloth soaked with alcohol. Eichmann drew his arm away. "It isn't necessary to give me an injection," he said. "I won't utter a sound . . . I promise."

"Don't worry," the doctor said. "It's nothing, just something to control your excitement." He moved to insert the needle.

"No, no . . . I'm not excited at all," Eichmann insisted.

"Please," Malkin said. "We have to do this. We have orders."

The hypodermic needle used by Yonah Elian to sedate Eichmann before the El Al flight.

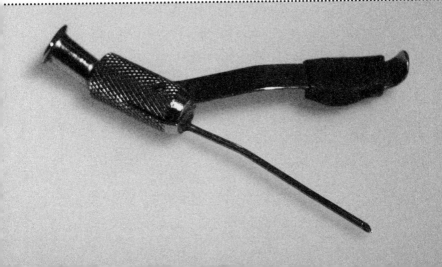

Eichmann gave in and laid his arm in his lap. The doctor slid the needle into a vein and attached a tube. Then he delivered the sedative. Eichmann soon faded, mumbling, "No, no. I don't need it."

"We're ready to travel," the doctor said, checking Eichmann's pulse.

Yaakov Gat and Rafi Eitan grasped Eichmann under the arms and carried him into the garage. He was conscious but barely able to speak. Looking drowsily at the others, all in their El Al uniforms, he said, "I don't look right. I have to put on a jacket." They had not given him one because it would have restricted access to his arm, but it was a good sign that he seemed to actually want to help. Maybe he would not resist at all while getting on the plane.

Gat climbed into the backseat of the limousine and drew Eichmann down beside him. Dr. Elian also sat in the back, ready to inject more sedative if needed. Yoel Goren took the passenger's seat, and Aharoni started the engine. Malkin pulled open the gate — he was staying behind at Tira in case there was trouble at the airport and the team needed to retreat to the house. Eitan and Tabor were to follow in another car. The limousine rolled out of the driveway and turned the corner.

At the same time, in a quiet corner of the Hotel Internacional lobby, Captain Wedeles assembled the El Al crew members who had yet to be informed of the true reason for the flight. The seven individuals included the radio operators, pursers, and flight attendants, all of whom had spent the past twenty-four hours enjoying Buenos Aires. They grew curious on seeing Yosef Klein and Adi Peleg standing beside Wedeles, and worried on seeing how serious the captain looked.

"We're advancing the return departure," Wedeles said. "Please be downstairs in an hour. No shopping. No nothing. After that, you're to stick with me. If I get up, you get up with me. If I sit down, you sit down, because I want you all around me at all times."

"You're participating in a great event," Peleg said. "Don't ask me what it is, but we're taking a very important person back to Israel with us. I will tell you his identity later on."

"We'll be boarding the plane in three cars at the maintenance area," Wedeles continued. "In one of the cars will be that man."

Aharoni took a long, circuitous route to the airport in order to avoid the checkpoints on the major roads. Eichmann was still and silent in the back — almost too still, too silent. They feared that he might be acting more drowsy than he actually was in order to fool them. Then, when his chance came — perhaps even while boarding the plane — he might scream out for help and jeopardize the operation.

The fake air crew ID card for "Zeev Zichroni," created by Shalom Dani.

At the airport's main entrance, the guards waved the car through without inspection because of its diplomatic plates. In the parking lot, they met Peleg and a minibus carrying the crew. Shalom was there as well. It was almost 11:00 P.M. Someone ran to alert Harel, and he came hurrying out of the terminal.

He glanced into the limousine. Eichmann appeared to be asleep. Dr. Elian assured Harel that he was able to see and hear, though not alert enough to know what was going on around him. Harel gave the order to move out to the plane.

Peleg took over the escort car that Eitan had driven to the airport. Shalom sat by his side in the passenger's seat. Both of them had gone in and out of the airport often enough to know the guards by their first names. They would lead the convoy through the gates into the maintenance area. Behind them was the limousine, driven by Aharoni, and last was the minibus with the plane's crew.

The line of vehicles approached the gate to the Aerolíneas Argentinas hangar, where the El Al plane waited. An armed sentry walked up to the first car and recognized Peleg and Shalom sitting inside. He raised the barrier and waved them forward, pleasantly shouting, "Hi, Israel!" The limousine and minibus rolled by slowly to give the guard a chance to look inside and see that everyone was wearing an El Al uniform.

"Be absolutely silent," Gat warned Eichmann as they neared the Britannia. "We're about to go onto the plane."

Eichmann remained listless, as if he didn't even hear the warning. The limousine stopped at the bottom of the stairs that led up to the plane. Captain Tohar opened the back door. Gat lifted Eichmann out. His legs had almost no strength, so Yoel Goren supported him from the other side.

The crew filed out of the minibus. "Form a circle around us and follow us," Eitan instructed them.

Gat and Goren hauled Eichmann up the stairs. His feet dangled limply, hitting each step in turn. An airport searchlight illuminated the gangway. Everyone was crowded closely together, making Eichmann all but indistinguishable in the mass of El Al uniforms.

Once on board, Gat and Goren led Eichmann to the back of the plane and placed him in a window seat in the first-class cabin. Gat sat down across the aisle, and Dr. Elian took the seat directly behind. A flight attendant covered Eichmann with a blanket.

"Pretend to sleep," Gat told everybody.

A purser lowered the overhead lights and drew a curtain across the first-class cabin entrance. If customs officers or the police searched the plane before takeoff, they would be told that the relief crew was getting some rest before the long flight.

At 11:15 P.M., the doors were locked closed, and Tohar fired the engines. Then he taxied to the terminal to pick up their remaining passengers.

In the terminal restaurant, Isser Harel felt the reverberations from the Britannia's engines against the window. He knew Eichmann was on board. Once the crew had gotten through customs and the Mossad agents who were returning on the flight had boarded as well, they would depart. Harel was eager for that moment to come. He still feared the police or a group of Nazis would rush into the airport at the last minute to stop the flight.

Harel left his restaurant headquarters and met up with Yosef Klein, who assured him that everything was ready. He then headed outside the terminal, where Eitan and Shalom had just arrived by car from the hangar. They reported that the transfer of Eichmann onto the plane had gone flawlessly. They were staying behind with Malkin to return the cars and clean up. Harel shook hands with each of them in turn, and the men wished one another luck on their journeys back to Israel.

Then Harel hurried into the passenger lounge, where he was joined by Aharoni and Tabor. Medad finally appeared, his car having broken down on the way to the airport. The agents all had piles of luggage with them.

Klein came up to Harel, his face stricken with worry. "You surprise me with this crowd!"

"They're all my people. Don't worry," Harel said.

At 11:30 P.M., Klein received word that the plane was ready for takeoff. However, there was still no sign of the customs and passport-control officers who were to check their papers and allow them to board. Since there were no other flights leaving at that late hour, it was unlikely that the officials were busy.

As midnight approached, Harel and Aharoni paced back and forth in the passenger lounge. Had someone seen them bringing Eichmann onto the plane? Had the airport been tipped off that there was something suspicious about the El Al flight? Harel considered sending word to Tohar to leave without him and the rest of the passengers, but then he calmed himself and gave it a few more minutes.

At last Klein found a customs official. The tall, heavily bearded officer walked into the lounge and apologized for the delay. From his sheepish grin, they knew it had merely been an oversight. The officer stamped everyone's passports, wishing each of them a hearty *Bon viaje!*

As Harel boarded the Britannia, he spotted a man in a suit running out of the terminal from another exit and speaking urgently with an airport official. The Mossad chief had a sinking feeling that something was wrong, but the plane doors shut behind him.

In the cockpit, Tohar finished the preflight checklist with his crew. After Harel sat down in the cockpit jump seat, Tohar ordered the flight engineer to start the engines. Following procedure, he radioed the control tower. "El Al is ready to taxi. Request clearance to Recife." Then he gave them the checkpoints and altitude that Shaul had provided for their false flight plan to Brazil.

The tower answered, "El Al, proceed to runway. Hold for takeoff clearance en route to Recife."

They were so close to being away, thought Harel. The man he had seen leaving the terminal was not important. Still, he wished they had already left Argentina far behind them.

Tohar released the brakes, and the Britannia moved forward to its takeoff position. The plane cleared the airport terminal. They were almost free.

But then the tower radioed a new message. "El Al, hold your position. There is an irregularity in the flight plan."

Everyone in the cockpit went still. Harel was sure that they had been caught. Tohar did not respond to the tower. Instead, he stopped the plane and turned around in his seat to see what Harel wanted to do.

"What happens if we ignore the tower's command and take off for Dakar?" Harel asked.

Tohar told him he could fly the Britannia low to the ground and evade the radar, head south instead of north to Recife, and throw any pursuers off for a while. He doubted that the Argentine air force was on standby, but if they took off without clearance, there was a chance that a fighter plane might be scrambled to force them down. Tohar was an Israeli air force reserve pilot, and he could do whatever needed to be done, but the risks were many.

"There's one more option," he said. "Before having the Argentine air force put on our tail, we should check and see if they really know that Adolf Eichmann is on board. Let's not create a problem that doesn't exist."

Harel nodded, even though he knew the longer they waited on the tarmac, the more time the authorities would have to alert the air force and prevent the Britannia from taking off.

Tohar turned to Shaul. "They are saying there's an irregularity in the flight plan. So let's send the guy who prepared it to the tower to find out what's going on. If you don't return in ten minutes, we'll take off without you."

CHAPTER 16

Yosef Klein paced the apron beside the airport terminal, confused as to why the plane had stopped. He had checked and rechecked *everything*. There was no reason the plane should not have departed, unless its secret passenger was known. Klein tried to make eye contact with someone in the cockpit, but nobody was moving, nor did they open a window to call out to him. After what felt like an age, he saw one of the pilots gesture for stairs to be brought to the plane's side. Then the doors opened, and Shaul stepped out.

Klein waited for him at the bottom of the steps. "What the hell is happening?"

"The tower wants something to do with the flight plan," Shaul said.

Klein knew it was highly unusual for a plane to be stopped and the navigator summoned out. This might be a trap.

"Shall I go with you?" Klein asked.

"No, wait. I'll do it alone."

Shaul hurried to the tower. He climbed the stairs slowly, like a man approaching the gallows.

"What is the problem?" he asked the controller in English, looking around for any sign of the police.

"There's a signature missing," the controller said, holding the flight plan up in his hand. "And what is your alternate route?"

Shaul relaxed. "Porto Alegre," he replied before adding the detail to the plan and signing the document. Then he rushed back down the steps. "Everything's okay. Something was missing on the flight plan," he said to Klein as he passed him.

In the cockpit, everybody sighed with relief when Shaul reported what had happened. The doors closed again, and Tohar called the tower. "This is El Al. May we proceed?"

"Affirmative."

At 12:05 A.M. on May 21, the plane rushed down the runway and lifted off. Once they had crossed out of Argentine airspace, excitement swept through the cabin. The "El Al crew" in first class rose from their seats, hugged one another, and cheered their success. Wedeles and the few other true crew members who already knew the special passenger's identity joined in the celebrations. The spontaneous outburst surprised Harel, and although he had hesitated to inform everyone else on the flight of the circumstances, it was clear now that secrecy was pointless.

Harel allowed Adi Peleg, the El Al security chief, to deliver the news: "You've been accorded a great privilege. You are taking part in an operation of supreme importance to the Jewish people. The man with us on the plane is Adolf Eichmann."

A shock wave of emotion followed his words. The flight attendant sitting next to Eichmann felt her heart sink. She stared in disbelief at this skinny, helpless man, nervously drawing on a cigarette, his Adam's apple bobbing up and down in fright. In disgust, she stood up and moved away.

In the cockpit, it was all business. The plane gained altitude, and Tohar steered due northeast across Uruguay and out over the Atlantic, following the course that Shaul had plotted to give them the best chance of reaching Dakar.

There were no computers or calculators at this point in aviation history, so navigation depended on charts, pencils, compasses, dividers, rulers, and lots of math. Once over the ocean, the flight engineer and the navigator figured out their position using the stars and a sextant that projected through a hatch in the flight-deck ceiling. A large almanac held details of the stars' positions throughout the year (and the sun and Venus for navigating by day) and enabled them to calculate their position in the sky every forty minutes. Once the calculations were complete, they were then rechecked by the other engineer and navigator. The calculations for each star shot meant they only had about five minutes' break before starting the process again.

Zvi Tohar, both of the navigators, and flight engineer Shimon Blanc had supervised the Britannia's proving flight between New York and Tel Aviv in late 1957. That journey had covered 5,760 miles in fifteen hours — the longest flight ever taken by a commercial airliner at that time — in a plane stripped of its seats, its galleys, and anything else deemed unnecessary, including passengers. The lack of weight meant that their fuel went a lot further. They had also had the benefit of a strong tailwind of roughly sixty-five miles per hour. For that flight, they figured the maximum still-air (no wind) range of the plane to be around 4,700 miles. The distance from Buenos Aires to Dakar was 4,650 miles. While they could expect some tailwinds along the route, they were still carrying some four tons of additional weight, and this meant they had to fly 2,000 to 3,000 feet lower than on the proving flight, consuming roughly 5 percent more fuel per hour.

There was no guarantee that the wind conditions would be to their advantage.

Shaul and Tohar were confident that they would reach Dakar, but they were also conscious that anything might happen to interfere with their plans. Over a thirteen- to fourteen-hour flight, slight deviations could add up to create big problems. At best they might be able to divert to another African airport — perhaps Abidjan in the Ivory Coast. At worst, they might run out of fuel over the Atlantic.

At half past midnight, Nick Eichmann learned from someone in his search party that an Israeli passenger plane had departed Buenos Aires for Recife. Nick was certain that his father was on board. With the help of a former SS man, he alerted a contact in the Brazilian secret service and asked him to intercept the plane when it landed in Recife — exactly the threat that the nonstop flight to Dakar aimed to counter.

Hour after hour passed as the El Al plane crossed the wide expanse of the Atlantic. It flew first toward the volcanic island of Trinidad, 680 miles east of Brazil, then north toward Dakar. Periodically, the radio operators listened in for new weather forecasts, the navigators made slight alterations in their route, and Harel popped his head into the cockpit to ask if everything was on track.

In his seat in the back of the plane, Adolf Eichmann continued to be as compliant as he had been in the safe house. The doctor had stopped giving him the sedative once they had boarded the plane, and he was still handcuffed and goggled, but Harel ordered Eichmann's guards to stay ready, fearing that he might attempt to kill himself. The prisoner smoked heavily and fidgeted constantly in his seat. Now that they were in flight, most of the crew kept their distance from him.

The morning after the Britannia departed, Yosef Klein wrapped up his El Al business in Buenos Aires and boarded a flight back to New York. There was no time for the sightseeing trip in Brazil he had planned on his journey out. His reward had been to see the taillights of the plane disappear into the night with Adolf Eichmann on board.

That same morning, Rafi Eitan, Peter Malkin, Avraham Shalom, and Shalom Dani woke up at Tira, relaxed for the first time in months. Their mission had gone well, and Eichmann was no longer their responsibility. Still, there were a few loose ends to tie up: They erased all trace of their presence in the various safe houses, burned or disposed of any material they did not plan on taking with them, and returned the last of their cars. The final task on the list was to get out of the country.

Dani was booked on a flight out of Argentina the next day, but, with the anniversary celebrations in full flow, there had been no flights available for Eitan, Malkin, or Shalom. They bought three tickets for an overnight train to Mendoza, on the Chilean border. From there they would take another train through the Andes to Santiago. Isser Harel had assured them that the announcement of Eichmann's capture would not be made until they were all safely back in Israel.

• • •

In the Britannia cockpit, red lights blinked furiously as the plane descended over the Atlantic toward Dakar. They had flown for close to thirteen hours and far beyond the 4,650 miles projected.

Date.	AIRCRAFT.		Captain.	Holder's Operating Capacity.	Journey or Nature of Flight	
	Type.	Markings.			From	To
19.5.60	AXAGA		TOHAR	R7	DAKAR	RECI
—"	—"		—"	—"	RECIFE	BUENOS
21.5.60	—"		—"	—"	BUENOS-AIRES	DAK
21.5.60	—"		—"	—"	DAKAR	LOD
24.5.60	4XAGC		W. KATZ	—"	LOD	ZURI
—"	—"		—"	—"	ZURICH	BRUS
—"	—"		—"	—"	BRUSSELS	ZURI
—"	—"		—"	—"	ZURICH	LOD
30.5.60	4XAGB		W. KATZ	—"	LOD	ROM
—"	—"		—"	—"	ROME	MUNI
—"	—"		—"	—"	MUNICH	VIEN

The navigator's logbook for the El Al flight.

Shaul had altered their flight path and altitude a number of times during their ocean crossing to find more favorable winds. Once, Tohar jokingly went through the cabin asking if anybody had a cigarette lighter because they needed all the fuel they could get.

Now the time for jokes had passed. The gauges flashed that the plane was dangerously low on fuel. If there was a problem in Dakar, if the runways were shut down for any reason, they would not have enough gas to fly around the airport while waiting for permission to land or to divert elsewhere. The cockpit

| | | FLYING TIMES | | | | Instrument Flying. | TOTALS Brought Forward |
parture	Arrival.	DAY. In Charge.	Second.	NIGHT. In Charge.	Second.		REMARKS.
							807.05
345	1005	6.20					*Special To· Buenos·Aires*
330	2100	7.30					— '' —
305	1615	13.10					— '' —
235	0510	11.35					*Adolf Eichmann* — '' —
630	1210	5.40					
300	1430	1.30					
525	1645	1.20					
730	2250	5.20					
100	1310	5.10					
415	1605	1.50					
550	1750	1.00					
		8134.30					TOTALS Carried Forward.

was silent, everyone focused on the task at hand. Tohar stared out the window, focused on the horizon.

Finally, he saw Dakar through the window. He lowered the landing wheels and decreased their altitude. A final few breathless moments passed before they made a smooth landing on the runway, thirteen hours and ten minutes after leaving Buenos Aires. Tohar shut down two of the engines as soon as he slowed the plane, unsure whether there was sufficient fuel even to taxi to the terminal.

Isser Harel congratulated the cockpit crew, but he was worried that the Argentine authorities might have contacted Dakar during their flight, warning them that they might be carrying a suspicious passenger. If this was the case, a thorough search of the plane could be expected. Elian injected Eichmann with more sedative, and Gat sat down next to him. A steward drew the curtain across the first-class cabin and turned off the lights.

While an airport services crew refueled the plane, two Senegalese health inspectors came on board. Gat heard someone speaking in French. He placed Eichmann's head on his shoulder and pretended to be asleep. The inspectors barely gave the cabin a second look.

The rest of the stopover went smoothly. The crew loaded more food, and Shaul and Hassin filed a flight plan to Rome, even though they were going straight to Tel Aviv. They had already plotted out a 4,500-mile, eleven-hour route. They knew that the tailwinds over the Mediterranean were much stronger than those in the South Atlantic, meaning that the journey would not test the plane's limits in quite the same way as the journey to Dakar had done.

One hour and twenty minutes after landing, they left Senegal. The plane flew up the west coast of Africa, then northeast to Spain, gathering speed from the tailwinds as it turned almost due east toward Italy.

The flight deck told air-traffic control in Rome that they would be heading on to Athens. They then flew southeast across the Mediterranean before announcing to the Athens air-traffic controllers that they would go straight to Tel Aviv. They crossed southern Greece, skirting Turkey, then shifted toward Israel.

When the plane was making its final approach toward Lod Airport near Tel Aviv, Harel washed his face, shaved, and put on clean clothes, preparing himself for the rush of activity that would greet his arrival. He informed his men of their duties on landing, then stared out the window, eager to see the Israeli coastline appear out of the early morning sky.

New York City

UNITED
STATES

ATLANTIC
OCEAN

GULF OF
MEXICO

CARIBBEAN SEA

EQUATOR

Recife

BRAZIL

Buenos Aires
Departure: Friday, May 20

PACIFIC
OCEAN

ARGENTINA

Distance: 4,650 miles
Flying time: 13 hours

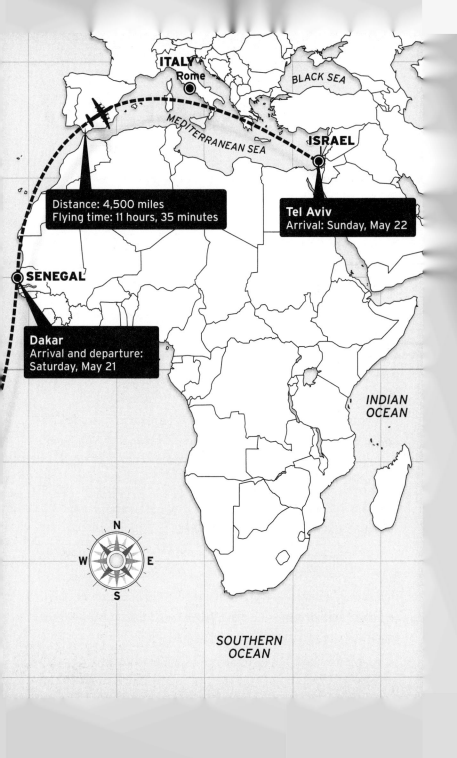

BLACK SEA

ITALY
Rome

MEDITERRANEAN SEA

ISRAEL

Distance: 4,500 miles
Flying time: 11 hours, 35 minutes

Tel Aviv
Arrival: Sunday, May 22

SENEGAL

Dakar
Arrival and departure:
Saturday, May 21

INDIAN
OCEAN

N
W   E
S

SOUTHERN
OCEAN

CHAPTER 17

Early on Sunday, May 22, Zvi Tohar lowered the landing gear on the plane. Fifteen minutes later, the wheels touched Israeli ground. There was no celebration as there had been when leaving Buenos Aires. The crew had been flying for almost twenty-four hours straight, and the agents watching Eichmann had not rested either. The mood in the aircraft was one of simple relief.

Tohar taxied to the terminal, where most of the crew disembarked. Harel made sure to shake everyone's hand as they left the plane. The captain also warmly thanked each of them as they stepped out. Then the doors were closed again, and Tohar taxied to the El Al service hangars, far from the terminal.

The moment they arrived, Harel left the plane and strode into one of the hangars, where he found a grease-smudged phone to ring Shin Bet headquarters. "The monster is in shackles," he told one of his lieutenants, then he ordered a vehicle. A short while later, a windowless black van appeared alongside the plane.

Tabor and Gat escorted a trembling, blindfolded Eichmann down the steps and into the back of the van. Harel explained to Gat that he was to take Eichmann to the secret Shin Bet detention center, which was located in an old Arab house on the edge of Jaffa. He then hurried toward Jerusalem, hoping to see David Ben-Gurion before his 10 A.M. cabinet meeting.

A secretary led him into the Prime Minister's office.

"I brought you a present," Harel said.

Ben-Gurion looked up from his paper-strewn desk, surprised to see him.

"I have brought Adolf Eichmann with me. For two hours now he has been on Israeli soil, and, if you authorize it, he will be handed over to the Israeli police."

Ben-Gurion remained silent for a few moments. "Are you positive it is Eichmann?"

It was not the response Harel expected, and he was slightly taken aback. "Of course I am positive. He even admitted it himself."

"Did anyone who met him in the past identify him?"

"No," Harel said.

"If that's the case, you have to find someone who knew him to go and inspect Eichmann in jail. Only after he has been officially identified will I be satisfied that this is the man."

Harel understood Ben-Gurion's caution, knowing the implications of any announcement he made. Even so, there was not a shred of doubt in his own mind that they had their man.

A few hours later, Moshe Agami, who had been a Jewish Agency representative during the war, was brought to Eichmann's cell. Agami had met Eichmann at the Palais Rothschild in Vienna in 1938, when the Nazi had made him stand to attention in his office while he pleaded for permission for the Jews to emigrate to Palestine. Agami confirmed Eichmann's identity. After he left, Benno Cohen, the former chairman of a Zionist organization in Germany in the mid-1930s, also identified the prisoner as Eichmann.

Harel phoned the Prime Minister and delivered the news. At last Ben-Gurion allowed himself to relish the operation's success. He wanted to announce the capture the next day. Harel asked him to wait — some of his agents were still in South America.

"How many people know Eichmann is in Israel?" Ben-Gurion asked.

Already more than fifty, Harel admitted.

"In that case, no waiting. We're going to announce!"

Early the next morning, May 23 — a blisteringly hot, cloudless Israeli day — Adolf Eichmann was brought in front of Judge Emanuel Halevi in Jaffa. When asked for his identity, he answered without hesitation, "I am Adolf Eichmann."

His voice cracking, Halevi charged him with the crime of genocide and issued his official arrest warrant.

In a restaurant in the center of Cologne, Fritz Bauer was waiting for an Israeli associate of Harel's, who had called an urgent meeting but who was now late. Bauer suspected something had gone terribly wrong with the Eichmann mission.

Harel's associate came into the restaurant and crossed quickly to the table. When Bauer heard the news of the capture, he leapt from his seat, tears welling in his eyes, and kissed the Israeli on both cheeks. Isser Harel had thought that the Hesse attorney general deserved to be told of the mission's success before it hit the headlines.

Now it was time for the rest of the world to know. At 4:00 P.M., David Ben-Gurion strode into the Knesset, Israel's parliament. Some had heard he had a special announcement, but no one had any idea what it might be. He stood at the podium, and the chamber hushed. In a solemn, strong voice he said, "I have to inform the Knesset that a short time ago one of the most notorious Nazi war criminals, Adolf Eichmann — who was

מדינת ישראל
الدولة الاسرائيلية

משפטים 8.

פקודת מאסר עד העמדה לדין
امر توقيف لحين المحاكمة

התובע
المدّعي

הנתבע
المدّعي عليه

בית המשפט
المحكمة

לכבוד פקיד בית האסורים
الى مدير سجن

מוסרים אנו לכ׳
نرسل اليكم

השם
الاسم

מספר המשפט
نمرة القضية

תאריך המאסר
تاريخ التوقيف

האשמה
التهمة

ניתן בחתימת ידי ביום .... לחודש 19
اعطي في اليوم

חתימת בית המשפט

חתימת השופט או שופט שלום ....
امضاء القاضي او حاكم الصلح

(ראה מעבר לדף)

א 196

responsible, together with the Nazi leaders, for what they called the 'Final Solution of the Jewish Question,' that is, the extermination of six million of the Jews of Europe — was discovered by the Israeli security services. Adolf Eichmann is already under arrest in Israel and will shortly be placed on trial in Israel under the terms of the law for the trial of Nazis and their helpers."

For a moment, everybody was rooted to their seats, unsure whether they had heard the Prime Minister correctly or that what he said was true. Slowly, they realized the enormity of his statement, and it was as if the air had been knocked from their chests.

"When they had recovered from the staggering blow," an Israeli journalist later reported, "a wave of agitation engulfed the hearers, agitation so deep that its likes had never before been known in the Knesset." Many went pale. One woman sobbed. Others jumped from their seats, needing to repeat aloud that Eichmann was in Israel in order to come to terms with the news. The parliamentary reporters ran to their booths.

Ben-Gurion stepped down and left the hall. Nobody was quite sure what to do as the chamber buzzed with the news. Eichmann. Captured. That was all anyone heard. Within hours, all of Israel and the rest of the world would be equally astonished by the historic announcement.

On May 25, Avraham Shalom was on a bus back to his hotel in Santiago, Chile. He had only just been able to send a cable to Mossad headquarters, notifying Isser Harel that he, Eitan, and Malkin were safe. They had arrived in the country three days earlier, after a breathtakingly beautiful journey by steam train from Mendoza through the Andes. On the day of their arrival, southern Chile had suffered a devastating earthquake, the most powerful ever recorded in the world, which had killed thousands and sent tsunamis surging across the Pacific.

Shalom looked idly over the shoulder of a passenger ahead of him, who was thumbing through a newspaper. There, in bold letters, he saw the word EICHMANN. Stunned, he stumbled off the bus at the next stop. At a corner stand, he bought a whole bundle of papers, most carrying the headline BEN-GURION ANNOUNCES THE CAPTURE OF ADOLF EICHMANN.

Shalom was livid. Nobody was supposed to know about the operation until they were all back in Israel. When he showed Eitan and Malkin the newspapers, they were equally angry, but there was nothing they could do about it. A few days later, they secured flights out of Chile. By chance, Shalom and Malkin were both routed through Buenos Aires, and they spent a worried hour on the tarmac at Ezeiza before takeoff.

At last they arrived home. Shalom discovered that his wife already knew he had been on the mission. Yaakov Gat had visited several days before to assure her that her husband was all right and would soon be home. Shalom knew that she would never utter a word about his involvement.

The others had similar experiences. On the evening of Ben-Gurion's announcement, Moshe Tabor was at the cinema with his wife when the film was interrupted by the news. Turning to him, she said, "You were in India, I thought?" Tabor tried to distract her, but she told him that she had noticed the toy pistol he brought home for their son was stamped MADE IN ARGENTINA.

At Peter Malkin's first family Sabbath dinner after his return, his brother talked of nothing else, wanting to know what had happened while Peter was in "Paris" for the past month. Malkin

A Holocaust survivor displays her Auschwitz tattoo as news of Eichmann's arrest breaks. The capture and trial would be a transformative moment for survivors to speak of what they experienced at the hands of the Nazis.

pleaded ignorance. His mother pushed him to say where he had really been.

"Look, didn't you get my letters?" he asked.

"They were like all your letters. They could have been written last year or tomorrow. . . . Were you involved with this?"

Malkin desperately wanted to tell her that he *had* been involved and that he had avenged his sister Fruma's death. "Please, Mama . . . Enough. I was in Paris."

Zvi Aharoni made the same excuse when his brother called him unexpectedly, wanting to know when he had returned to Israel. "I'm not naive," his brother said. "I know you were away for over two months, and I heard Ben-Gurion on the radio. I can add two and two together. Or can I? Well done!"

A Shin Bet secretary, who had also tied Aharoni's absence to the news, threw her arms around him on his first day back in the office. No words were needed.

CHAPTER 18

Outside Haifa, at a fortified police station code-named Camp Iyar, Adolf Eichmann sat in a ten-by-thirteen-foot cell. The lights overhead were never switched off, and a guard stayed with him at all times. Another guard kept watch through an opening in the reinforced door to make sure there was no contact between the guard inside and the prisoner.

The prison commandant feared not only that Eichmann might commit suicide but also that there might be an attempt on his life. His food was always tasted before serving, and his guards were carefully selected so that none of them had lost a family member in the Holocaust.

In Israel, the shock over the capture developed rapidly from pride in the mission's success to demands for swift revenge to a more settled view that justice could be delivered only in terms of the letter of the law. Ben-Gurion never wavered from his intentions. "The Jewish state is the heir of the six million murdered, the only heir." In his view, the trial should be held in Israel to fulfill that country's "historic duty" to those who were killed. As for the half million Israelis who were Holocaust survivors, the majority agreed with their leader.

The capture also had international implications. The Argentine government was outraged as soon as press reports revealed that "Israeli agents" had made the capture on Argentine soil. On June 1, the Argentine Foreign Minister, Diógenes Taboada, summoned Israeli Ambassador Arieh Levavi to demand an official explanation and the return of Eichmann.

"I don't think this is possible," Levavi said.

Two days later, Israeli diplomats sent a communiqué to the Argentines explaining that a group of "Jewish volunteers, including some Israelis," had captured Eichmann. These volunteers had "made contact" with the Nazi in Buenos Aires and had received his written permission to take him to Israel, where they had handed him over to the Israeli security services. The letter stated that Israel regretted if these volunteers had violated Argentine law but also asked that the "special significance of bringing to trial the man responsible for the murder of millions of persons belonging to the Jewish people be taken into account."

Some in Argentina were eager to punish the Israelis. Unable to strike against them directly, right-wing groups took their revenge on the local Jewish community. Tacuara carried out the worst of these attacks, beating up several Jewish students at the University of Buenos Aires and chanting, "Long live Eichmann. Death to Jews." One student was shot, and later, in a vicious assault, Tacuara radicals branded a swastika onto the chest of a teenage girl whose father was suspected of having helped the Israelis. Nick and Dieter Eichmann hung a swastika flag in front of their Garibaldi Street house and talked tough.

Vera Eichmann called upon the Argentine courts to instigate proceedings against those involved in her husband's kidnapping. On July 12, a judge approved the case and launched an investigation, aided by the Argentine security services.

By the fall, relations between Argentina and Israel had improved, and Vera Eichmann's case faltered. The inquiry met with resistance, no doubt because of the embarrassment of the Argentine police and security forces over having been outwitted. Investigators had failed to find out even the names of those who had returned on the El Al flight. The Mossad had covered its tracks well.

In the valley below the Old City of Jerusalem stands Beit Ha'am, the House of the People, a four-story white stone and marble auditorium in the heart of the modern, chaotic metropolis. On the morning of April 11, 1961, one hundred police and military guards with automatic weapons surrounded the building. At 8:55 A.M., Adolf Eichmann, dressed in a dark-blue suit and tie and wearing thick horn-rimmed glasses, was brought into the courtroom and placed in a bulletproof glass booth. He sat facing the empty witness stand. Two guards stood directly behind him.

The 750 spectators, who were already seated, gazed at Eichmann with unblinking eyes. In front of them, on the first level of a three-stepped dais, were the five prosecutors and two defense attorneys in their black gowns, seated at tables, side by side. Above them were the court stenographers and clerks. Cameras and microphones recorded every moment for the world to see and hear.

For five minutes, there was little movement in the hall. Eichmann sat like a statue, looking down at his shoes. There was muffled conversation as people attempted to understand how this man, with his ordinary face and measured demeanor, could be responsible for so much suffering.

When instructed by the judges in Hebrew, Eichmann turned toward them, his jaw cocked, his face fixed in a slight scowl.

"Adolf Eichmann, rise!"

Eichmann snapped to his feet the instant the judge's words were translated through his headset.

"Are you Adolf Eichmann, son of Adolf Karl Eichmann?"

"Yes," he answered.

The presiding judge, Moshe Landau, began reading the indictment, head down, hands together as if in prayer.

"First count. Nature of Offense: Crime against the Jewish People. Particulars of the Offense: (a) The Accused, during the period from 1939 to 1945, together with others, caused the deaths of millions of Jews as the persons who were responsible for the implementation of the plan of the Nazis for the physical extermination of the Jews, a plan known by its title 'The Final Solution of the Jewish Question.' "

Landau's indictment went on for an hour: fifteen counts, numerous charges within each. Eichmann had uprooted whole populations. He had assembled Jews in ghettos and deported them en masse. He had committed mass murder at the extermination camps of Auschwitz, Chelmno, Belzec, Sobibor, Treblinka, and Majdanek. He had enslaved Jews in forced labor camps and had denied their rights as human beings. He had inflicted inhuman torture and suffering. He had plundered the property of Jews through robbery, terror, and torture. He had operated across Europe as well as in the Soviet Union and the Baltic countries Lithuania, Latvia, and Estonia — always, always, with the intention of "destroying the Jewish People."

When the judge asked for Eichmann's plea of guilty or not guilty, he answered with the same phrase for each count. "In the sense of the indictment, no."

The defendant, Adolf Eichmann, standing in a bulletproof dock.

Attorney General Gideon Hausner, a man of stout figure and hooded blue eyes, followed the indictment with his opening speech. Hausner knew he was speaking for history.

When I stand before you here, Judges of Israel, to lead the Prosecution of Adolf Eichmann, I am not standing alone. With me are six million accusers. But they cannot rise to their feet and point an accusing finger towards him who sits in the dock and cry: "I accuse."

For their ashes are piled up on the hills of Auschwitz and the fields of Treblinka and are strewn in the forests of Poland. Their graves are scattered throughout the length and breadth of Europe. Their blood cries out, but their voice is not heard. Therefore I will be their spokesman.

The trial had begun. For the next fifty-six days, Hausner presented the case against Eichmann. It was as much about laying bare the Nazi program to exterminate the Jews as it was about prosecuting a single man. Throughout the prosecution, Eichmann remained composed and alert. Every time he entered his booth before a session, he wiped his desk and chair with a handkerchief, then arranged his papers about him as if he were preparing for a day at the office. Usually, he kept his eyes focused on the prosecutor.

On May 28, Zeev Sapir walked to the witness stand. After the war, Zeev had returned to Hungary, but he soon realized that there was nothing left for him there. He went to Palestine and joined the fight for an independent Israeli state. Later, he married and started a family, working as a teacher.

It was difficult for Zeev to speak of the past, but he had never forgotten it. On his way into the chamber, he felt a rush of pride and elation at seeing the enemy of his people sitting between two Israeli guards. After a judge swore Zeev in, the young assistant prosecutor Gabriel Bach began his questions. The first were simple: name, town of birth, date the Germans arrived. Then he was asked about the clearing of Dobradovo.

"How many Jews were you in your village?" Bach asked.

"One hundred and three souls, including children of all ages," Zeev said.

Bach then asked when Zeev had heard that an important SS officer was expected in Munkács. Zeev described the roll call and the man named Eichmann coming into the ghetto at the head of a party of German and Hungarian officers.

"You see the accused here. Can you identify him as the man whom you saw then?"

Again Zeev looked to Eichmann, who sat in his booth, eyes down at his desk, writing something in his notebook. The name was the same, but the man across from Zeev was missing the uniform, the weapon, and the aura of power. What was more, seventeen years had passed. "It is hard to compare," Zeev said. "He's different from what he was, but there is some resemblance that I can see in him." He then told them about the horrors that had awaited him after Eichmann had left the camp. The memories were still raw.

During the retelling, Zeev felt faint on the witness stand. A clerk brought him a chair. He sat down uneasily and held his bowed head in his hands. He did not touch the glass of water offered to him.

Zeev Sapir testifies against Adolf Eichmann.

The prosecutor said he didn't need to continue, but Zeev wanted to tell his story. He had earned the right. He recounted the selection process at Auschwitz, the march from the coal mines, SS officer Lausmann and the pot, the indiscriminate shootings in the forest. When he had finished speaking, Zeev raised his sleeve and showed the courtroom his Auschwitz tattoo: A3800.

It was impossible to know what role his testimony would play in the trial's outcome, but the important thing for Zeev Sapir was that the facts of what he had experienced because of Adolf Eichmann were now known. Indeed, given the exhaustive coverage of the trial in the newspapers and on radio and television, Zeev's story was broadcast across the globe.

Several of the agents who captured Eichmann came to see him in his glass booth. Most didn't bother with more than one session; they were busy with other operations. It was enough to know that they had succeeded in bringing Eichmann to justice.

Once Hausner finished presenting his case, the defense took over, arguing that the Nazi state had been responsible for the crimes, not Eichmann. He claimed he had merely followed orders and that his role in the widespread atrocities was limited at best.

Finally, Eichmann spoke in his own defense. Given his clipped, military tone, one might have expected straightforward answers, but instead he was long-winded and often contradicted himself. He was unmoved by Attorney General Hausner's many attempts to force him into an admission of legal guilt. Still, he could not deny the weight of evidence against him.

After closing statements on August 14, the judges adjourned the trial to weigh their decision. Four months later, they returned with their verdict. Eichmann was found guilty on all counts of the indictment, but he was acquitted on several individual charges within these counts. As he listened to the judgment, Eichmann's face twitched, and he looked frantically from side to side. There was no avoiding the truth now.

On December 15, 1961, Judge Landau asked Eichmann to rise, and delivered the sentence:

> For the dispatch of each train by the accused to Auschwitz, or to any other extermination site, carrying 1,000 human beings, meant that the accused was a direct accomplice in 1,000 premeditated acts of murder ... Even if we had found that the accused acted out of blind obedience, as he argued, we would still have said that a man who took part in crimes of such magnitude as these over years must pay the maximum penalty known to the law ... But we have found that the accused acted out of an inner identification with the orders that he was given and out of a fierce will to achieve the criminal objective ... This Court sentences Adolf Eichmann to death.

It was the first — and to this day only — sentence of death by an Israeli court.

Eichmann stood absolutely still, his lips drawn together as if he were pressing a stone tightly between them. His throat and the collar of his shirt were soaked with sweat. Eight minutes after the session began, the bailiff called, "All rise!" and the judges left the courtroom. The trial was over.

Eichmann appealed the judgment, but on May 29, 1962, it was denied. He flushed with anger when the five-judge panel restated

Eichmann stands to hear the verdict read by Judge Moshe Landau.

the reason for the guilty verdict. His request for clemency to the Israeli President was also denied, and on May 30, the judges informed Eichmann that he would be hanged at midnight.

In his cell, he asked for a bottle of white wine, cigarettes, and a paper and pen. He wrote a final letter to his wife and sons in Argentina. Then he shaved, dressed in brown slacks and a shirt, and brushed his teeth.

There was no final-hour confession or plea for mercy from Eichmann.

Two guards and Arye Nir, the prison commandant, entered the cell. Before they bound his hands behind his back, Eichmann requested a moment to pray. He retreated to a corner for a minute and then announced, "I am ready."

The guards escorted him down the prison corridor. The group entered the makeshift execution chamber through a hole that had been knocked in one of the concrete walls. A wooden platform had been built over another hole cut in the floor. A rope hung from an iron frame above it.

Rafi Eitan stood in the room, ready to be one of the witnesses to the execution. Over the past few months, Eitan had interrogated Eichmann several times, gathering information about how the SS had been organized and operated. Eichmann stared at Eitan and said sharply, "I hope, very much, that it will be your turn soon after mine."

The guards placed Eichmann on a trapdoor on the platform and tied his legs together. A white hood was brought out, but Eichmann refused it. He looked at the four journalists selected to witness the execution as they scribbled on their pads. A coiled rope was placed over his head.

"Long live Germany," he declared. "Long live Argentina. Long live Austria . . . I had to obey the laws of war and my flag. I am ready."

Two guards moved behind the curtain of blankets that shielded the trapdoor release mechanism from the prisoner. There were two buttons, only one of which was connected, so the guards would never know which of them had opened the trapdoor.

Eichmann smiled thinly and called out, "Gentlemen, we shall meet again soon, so is the fate of all men. I have believed in God all my life, and I die believing in God."

It was exactly midnight. The commandant yelled, "Ready!"

Eichmann half closed his eyes, looking down at the trapdoor underneath his feet. His face was ashen.

"Action!"

The two guards hit their buttons, and the platform opened with a clang. Eichmann fell ten feet into the room below without a sound. The rope went straight, snapped, and then swayed back and forth. A doctor moved into the chamber, took Eichmann's pulse, and declared the Nazi dead.

Guards cut down the body from the noose. The face of the corpse was white, and the rope had cut into its neck. As one of the guards, Shlomo Nagar, lifted the body, he expelled some air from its lungs, producing a sound that almost made him faint, and that he would hear in his nightmares for years to come.

The guards placed the body on a stretcher, covered it with a gray wool blanket, and carried it through the prison yard and out of the gates into a clearing in an orange grove. A mist hung in the air. A man who had once worked at an extermination-camp crematorium was already there, firing the furnace. As the guards placed the body into the smoldering oven, one of them lost his balance, and the corpse fell to the ground.

Everyone froze.

One of the witnesses, Michael Goldmann, who had been the Chief Inspector of the police unit that collected evidence for the trial, rolled up his sleeves and stepped forward to pick up the corpse and put it inside the furnace. In the fiery glow, the Auschwitz tattoo on his arm was clearly visible. Goldmann's parents and his ten-year-old sister had been killed at the extermination camp.

Two hours later, the ashes were scooped out of the furnace. They filled half of a small nickel canister. Goldmann considered how many Jews must have made up the mountains of ashes outside the Auschwitz-Birkenau crematoriums. In the wintertime, the SS guards had forced him to spread those ashes on the paths so that they would not slip on the ice.

Now Nir, Goldmann, and Rev. William Hull, a Canadian Protestant missionary who had also witnessed the execution, drove to the port of Jaffa with the canister. They arrived just before daybreak on June 1. Several other observers were waiting. They motored into the open sea in a police patrol boat. Six miles out, just beyond Israeli territorial waters, the captain shut off the engines. The boat drifted in the darkness, rising and falling in the swells. A sliver of red light appeared on the horizon.

As Hull said a prayer to himself, Nir walked to the back of the boat and emptied the canister into the swirling waves. The ashes drifted up on the crest of a wave, then disappeared. By casting the ashes into the sea, the Israeli government had ensured there would be no place for any monument or shrine to Adolf Eichmann.

The engines were restarted, and the captain steered back to the coast. They reached the shore just as the sun was rising in the sky.

EPILOGUE

The Eichmann trial was almost more important in the field of education than in that of justice. David Ben-Gurion achieved his ambition: The trial educated the Israeli public, particularly the young, about the true nature of the Holocaust. And, after sixteen years of silence, it allowed survivors to openly share their experiences.

In the rest of the world, the intense media coverage and the wave of Eichmann biographies and fantastic accounts of his

Jews in Jerusalem listen to Eichmann's trial on a portable radio.

capture rooted the Holocaust in the collective cultural consciousness. The Shoah, as it was also known, was not to be forgotten, and an outpouring of survivor memoirs, scholarly works, plays, novels, documentaries, paintings, museum exhibits, and films followed in the wake of the trial and still continues today. This consciousness, in Israel and throughout the world, is the enduring legacy of the operation to capture Adolf Eichmann.

As for the Eichmann family, Vera and her youngest son, Ricardo, moved back and forth between Buenos Aires and West Germany for several years before settling in Osterburken, forty miles west of Heidelberg, in West Germany. Vera never accepted that her husband was guilty of his crimes, nor did she get over his execution. Ricardo scarcely remembers his father, and the Eichmann name is a weight that he continues to carry. Now a professor of archaeology in Germany, he recognizes the terrible deeds of Adolf Eichmann and is reluctant to speak about him. Of the three older sons, Horst continues to live in Buenos Aires and is reportedly a neo-Nazi leader. Dieter and Nick moved back to Germany, to Lake Constance, on the Rhine. They remain convinced that their father just obeyed orders and that most of what was said against him at the trial was false. Beyond that, they do not wish to discuss him.

Fritz Bauer, whose involvement remained a secret for two decades, moved quickly on the cases of other war criminals already under investigation. In the weeks after Ben-Gurion's announcement, Bauer and his fellow West German prosecutors arrested a host of former Nazis implicated in the atrocities, including several of Eichmann's deputies. Right up to his death in 1968, the Hesse Attorney General cracked down on German fascist groups and campaigned vigorously to unseat former Nazis from power.

Simon Wiesenthal won a tremendous amount of attention for his contribution to the hunt for Adolf Eichmann. Encouraged by the renewed public interest in war crimes, he returned to hunting Nazis and spent forty-five years promoting "justice, not vengeance."

Before the operation to catch Eichmann unfolded, Sylvia Hermann left Argentina for the United States, where she still lives today. In 1971, Lothar Hermann received a reward from Israel for information leading to the arrest of Eichmann. Until then, his and his daughter's role in the capture had been kept a secret.

For the Mossad agents whose families had been devastated by the Nazis, their participation carried an even greater personal satisfaction. In 1967, while on a job in Athens, Malkin received a call from Avraham Shalom, who told him that Malkin's mother had been rushed to the hospital. Malkin returned to Tel Aviv on the first flight out and went straight to her bedside. Her eyes were closed, her face ashen. He tried to speak to her, but it didn't seem like she heard him.

"She can't talk," said the old woman in the neighboring bed.

"Mama," Malkin whispered in her ear, "I want to tell you something. What I promised, I have done. I got Eichmann."

His mother did not open her eyes, nor did she turn her head. It had been seven years since Malkin had grabbed Eichmann on Garibaldi Street. He had kept the secret from her because of the oath he had sworn, but now he could not bear for her to die without knowing what he had accomplished.

"Mama, Fruma was avenged. It was her own brother who captured Adolf Eichmann."

"She can't hear you," said the old woman, growing impatient with his visit.

Just as he was losing hope, Malkin felt a hand cover his, and then his mother grasped his hand tightly.

"Do you understand?" Malkin asked her.

Her eyes fluttered open. "Yes," she said. "I understand."

My Sister Fruma, a painting Peter Malkin completed while guarding Eichmann.

Author's Note

Two decades ago, while studying abroad in college, I first heard of Adolf Eichmann. In Luxembourg, a Holocaust survivor explained that she was never able to speak of her terrible experiences during the war until after the famous Eichmann trial in Jerusalem. In a way, she felt the testimonies by many survivors at the trial gave her permission to speak of her own suffering. Yes, the story of the Eichmann capture is a great spy tale, with lots of twists and turns, but in the scheme of history — and in so many personal lives — it is important as well. That's why I wrote this book.

Researching the story was an incredible journey, one that found me on four continents, interviewing Mossad spies in Tel Aviv, Israel; tracking down former Nazis in Buenos Aires, Argentina; and unearthing rarely seen archives in Germany and elsewhere. Along the way, a crack team of researchers and translators helped me. With one-on-one talks with many of the key individuals in the operation, some of whom had never before been interviewed, I was able to put together what I hope is the most accurate account of these dramatic events. Over the course of the research, I also discovered some important documents, including the passport Eichmann used to escape Europe after the war.

Now, despite my best efforts, my reconstruction of these events is no doubt imperfect. First of all, this is a spy story, and some elements of what exactly happened remain secret — and/or clouded in half-truths. Second, my interview subjects often contradicted one another on specific versions of events. I've tried my best to reconcile conflicting accounts, and in the Notes section of the book, I pinpoint a few of these instances. Every writer of history wishes he could work with perfect, complete information, but in the end, we simply have to unearth as much as we can and then make do with that.

I made do with a great deal thanks to the efforts of many people who assisted me. A special shout-out in particular to my researchers Valeria Galvan, Nava Mizrahi, and Franziska Ramson. Many individuals spoke to me in the course of my interviews, but special acknowledgments to Avraham Shalom and Shaul Shaul, who suffered my barrage of questions the longest. Finally, thanks to Liz O'Donnell, who walks through fire with me on every book, and to Cheryl Klein, my sharp-penned, incredibly talented editor at Scholastic.

Bibliography

Asterisks indicate titles of the most interest and accessibility for young-adult readers.

Archives and Libraries
Archiv der Sozialen Demokratie der Friedrich-Ebert-Stiftung, Bonn.
Archivo General de la Nación, Buenos Aires.
Avraham Harman Institute of Contemporary Jewry, Oral History Division, Hebrew University, Jerusalem.
Biblioteca National, Buenos Aires.
Bundesarchiv, Koblenz.
Central Zionist Archives, Jerusalem.
Columbia University Library, New York.
Dirección Nacional de Migraciones, Buenos Aires.
Hessisches Hauptstaatsarchiv, Wiesbaden.
Israel State Archives, Jerusalem.
Massuah Institute for the Study of the Holocaust, Kibbutz Tel Itzhak, Israel.
National Archives and Records Administration, Washington, DC.
New York Public Library, New York.
New York University Library, New York.
Steven Spielberg Jewish Film Archive, Hebrew University, Jerusalem.
Tribunales Federales de Comodoro Py, Buenos Aires.
United States Holocaust Memorial Museum, Washington, D.C.
Yad Vashem, Jerusalem.
YIVO Institute for Jewish Research, New York.

Documentary Interviews and Materials
The Hunt for Adolf Eichmann, directed by Dan Setton, 1998. Interview transcripts of Zvi Aharoni, Manus Diamant, Michael Gilead, Isser Harel, Peter Malkin, Moshe Tabor, and Elie Wiesel.
I Met Adolf Eichmann, directed by Clara Glynn, 2003. Interview transcripts of Zvi Aharoni, Martha Eggers, Michael Gilead, Otto Lindhorst, Heinz Lühr, Shlomo Nagar, Zeev Sapir, Ursula Schulze, Moshe Tabor, Roberto Tonet, and Ruth Tramer.

Author Interviews
Roberto Alemann, Dan Alon, Shmuel Alony, anonymous Tacuara members, Angolina Bascelli, Rafi Eitan, Yaakov Gat, Amelia Hahn, Oved Kabiri, Yosef

Klein, Anthony Kleinert, Dr. Leonhardt, Arye Levavi, Jose Moskoviz, Dr. Ernesto Palenzola, Pedro Probierzym, Saskia Sassen, Daniel Sasson, Shamri Shabtai, Avraham Shalom, Shaul Shaul, Baruch Tirosh, and Luba Volk.

Books and Articles

Aarons, Mark, and John Loftus. *Unholy Trinity: How the Vatican's Nazi Networks Betrayed Western Intelligence to the Soviets.* New York: St. Martin's Press, 1991.

Aharoni, Zvi. *On Life and Death: The Tale of a Lucky Man.* London: Minerva, 1998.

Aharoni, Zvi, and Wilhelm Dietl. *Operation Eichmann: The Truth About the Pursuit, Capture and Trial of Adolf Eichmann.* London: Orion, 1998.

Anderson, Jack. *Peace, War, Politics: An Eyewitness Account.* New York: Forge, 2000.

*Arendt, Hannah. *Eichmann in Jerusalem: A Report on the Banality of Evil.* New York: Penguin Books, 1987.

Aschenauer, Rudolf. *Ich, Adolf Eichmann: Ein historischer Zeugenbericht.* Augsburg: Druffel-Verlag, 1980. A distilled version of the Sassen transcripts.

Bar-Zohar, Michael. *The Avengers.* New York: Hawthorn Books, 1968.

——. *Ben-Gurion: A Biography.* Tel Aviv: Biblioteka-Aliia, 1987.

——. *Spies in the Promised Land: Iser Harel and the Israeli Secret Service.* Boston: Houghton Mifflin, 1972.

Ben-Natan, Asher. *The Audacity to Live: An Autobiography.* Tel Aviv: Mazo, 2007.

Black, Ian, and Morris Benny. *Israel's Secret Wars: A History of Israel Intelligence.* London: Hamish Hamilton, 1991.

Black, Peter R. *Ernst Kaltenbrunner: Ideological Soldier of the Third Reich.* Princeton, NJ: Princeton University Press, 1984.

Bower, Tom. *Blind Eye to Murder: Britain, America and the Purging of Nazi Germany — A Pledge Betrayed.* London: Andre Deutsch, 1981.

Boyle, Kay. *Breaking the Silence: Why a Mother Tells Her Son About the Nazi Era.* New York: Institute of Human Relations Press, 1962.

Braham, Randolph L. *The Politics of Genocide: The Holocaust in Hungary.* New York: Columbia University Press, 2000.

Breitman, Richard, et al. *U.S. Intelligence and the Nazis.* New York: Cambridge University Press, 2005.

Briggs, Emil. *Stand Up and Fight.* London: George G. Harrap, 1972.

Bukey, Evan Burr. *Hitler's Hometown: Linz, Austria, 1908–1945.* Bloomington, IN: Indiana University Press, 1986.

*Cesarani, David. *Becoming Eichmann: Rethinking the Life, Crimes, and Trial of a "Desk Murderer."* New York: Da Capo Press, 2006.

Clarke, Comer. *Eichmann: The Man and His Crime.* New York: Ballantine Books, 1960.

Deacon, Richard. *The Israeli Secret Service.* London: Hamish Hamilton, 1977.

Derogy, Jacques, and Hesi Carmel. *The Untold History of Israel*. New York: Grove Press, 1979.

Diamant, Manus. Manuscript. Massuah Archives, Israel.

Douglas, Lawrence. *The Memory of Judgment: Making Law and History in the Holocaust*. New Haven, CT: Yale University Press, 2001.

Eban, Abba. *Personal Witness*. New York: G. P. Putnam's Sons, 1993.

Eichmann, Adolf. *Meine Flucht*. Hessisches Hauptstaatsarchiv, Alliierte Prozesse, 6/247, folder 1.

"The Eichmann Chase." *Newsweek*, July 25, 1960.

"Eichmann Memoirs." National Archives and Records Administration, CIA Records Search Tool.

Erez, Tsvi. "Hungary: Six Days in July 1944." *Holocaust and Genocide Studies* 3, no. 1 (1988): 37–53.

Fried, Tal. "Official Israeli Institutions in Pursuit of Nazi War Criminals, 1945–60." PhD diss., University of Haifa, 2002.

Friedman, Tuviah. *The Blind Man Who Discovered Adolf Eichmann in Argentina*. Haifa: Institute of Documentation in Israel, 1987.

——. *The Hunter*. Edited and translated by David C. Gross. Haifa: Institute of Documentation in Israel, 1961.

Fulbrook, Mary. *German National Identity After the Holocaust*. Cambridge: Polity Press, 1999.

*Goñi, Uki. *The Real Odessa: How Perón Brought the Nazi War Criminals to Argentina*. London: Granta, 2003.

Guri, Haim. *Facing the Glass Booth: The Jerusalem Trial of Adolf Eichmann*. Detroit, MI: Wayne State University Press, 2004.

Gutman, Daniel. *Tacuara: Historia de la Primera Guerrilla Urbana Argentina*. Buenos Aires: Vergara Grupo Zeta, 2003.

Gutman, Yisrael, and Michael Berenbaum, eds. *Anatomy of the Auschwitz Death Camp*. Bloomington, IN: Indiana University Press, 1994.

Haim, Avni. "Jewish Leadership in Times of Crisis: Argentina During the Eichmann Affair." In *Studies in Contemporary Jewry*, ed. Peter Medding, vol. 11, *Values, Interests and Identity*, pp. 117–23. New York: Oxford University Press, 1995.

Harel, Isser. *House on Garibaldi Street*. London: Frank Cass, 1997.

Hausner, Gideon. *Justice in Jerusalem*. New York: Harper & Row, 1966.

Höttl, Wilhelm. *The Secret Front: The Story of Nazi Political Espionage 1938–1945*. London: Weidenfeld & Nicolson, 1953.

Hull, William L. *The Struggle for a Soul*. New York: Doubleday, 1963.

"Interview with Klaus Eichmann." *Quick*, January 1966.

Kurzman, Dan. *Ben-Gurion: Prophet of Fire*. New York: Simon & Schuster, 1983.

Lauryssens, Stan. *The Eichmann Diaries*. Unpublished English-language version provided by author.

Lawson, Colin. "Eichmann's Wife Speaks." *Daily Express*, December 12, 1961.

Lengyel, Olga. *Five Chimneys: The Story of Auschwitz*. New York: Howard Fertig, 1995.

Levai, Eugene. *Black Book on the Martyrdom of Hungarian Jewry*. Zurich: Central European Times, 1948.

Lévai, Jenö, ed. *Eichmann in Hungary: Documents*. New York: Howard Fertig, 1987.

*Levi, Primo. *Survival in Auschwitz: The Nazi Assault on Humanity*. New York: Collier Books, 1961.

Levy, Alan. *The Wiesenthal File*. London: Constable, 1993.

Lozowick, Yaacov. *Hitler's Bureaucrats: The Nazi Security Police and the Banality of Evil*. New York: Continuum, 2002.

Malkin, Peter Z. *The Argentina Journal*. New York: VWF Publishing, 2002.

Malkin, Peter and Harry Stein. *Eichmann in My Hands*. New York: Warner Books, 1990.

Marty, Kenneth. "Neo-Fascist Irrationality or Fantastic History? Tacuara, the Andinia Plan and Adolf Eichmann in Argentina." PhD diss., Princeton University, 1996.

McKechnie, Gary, and Nancy Howell. "Double Exposure." *Orlando*, December 1988.

Meding, Holger. *Flücht vor Nürnberg? Deutsch und Osterreichische Einwanderung in Argentinien*, 1945–1955. Cologne: Böhlau Verlag, 1992.

Mendelsohn, John, and Donald S. Detweiler, eds. *The Holocaust*. 18 vols. New York: Garland, 1982.

Mermelstein, Mel. *By Bread Alone: The Story of A-4685*. Los Angeles: Crescent Publications, 1979.

Mulisch, Harry. *Criminal Case 40/61: The Trial of Adolf Eichmann*. Philadelphia: University of Philadelphia Press, 2005.

Muller, Filip. *Eyewitness Auschwitz: Three Years in the Gas Chambers*. New York: Stein & Day, 1979.

Musmanno, Michael. *The Eichmann Kommandos*. Philadelphia: Macrae Smith, 1961.

Nagy-Talavera, Nicholas. *The Green Shirts and the Others: A History of Fascism in Hungary and Romania*. Oxford: Center for Romanian Studies, 2001.

Newton, Ronald. *The "Nazi Menace" in Argentina, 1931–47*. Palo Alto, CA: Stanford University Press, 1992.

Papadatos, Peter. *The Eichmann Trial*. New York: Praeger, 1964.

Pearlman, Moshe. *The Capture of Adolf Eichmann*. London: Weidenfeld & Nicolson, 1961.

Pick, Hella. *Simon Wiesenthal: A Life in Search of Justice*. Boston: Northeastern University Press, 1996.

Prittie, Terence. *Konrad Adenauer, 1876–1967*. Ann Arbor, MI: Tom Stacey, 1972.

Rathkolb, Oliver, ed. *Revisiting the National Socialist Legacy*. Innsbruck: Studien Verlag, 2004.

Rein, Raanan. *Argentina, Israel, and the Jews: Peron, the Eichmann Capture and After*. Bethesda, MD: University Press of Maryland, 2003.

Reynolds, Quentin, with Zwy Aldouby and Ephraim Katz. *Minister of Death: The Adolph Eichmann Story*. New York: Viking Press, 1961.

Robinson, Jacob. *And the Crooked Shall Be Made Straight: The Eichmann Trial, the Jewish Catastrophe, and Hannah Arendt's Narrative*. New York: Macmillan, 1965.

Sassen Transcripts. Collection of Robert Servatius. Hessisches Hauptstaatsarchiv, Alliierte Prozesse, 6/95–111.

Shpiro, Shlomo. *Geheimdienste in der Weltgeschichte: Spionage und verdeckte Aktionen von der Antike bis zur Gegenwart*. Munich: Verlag C. H. Beck, 2003.

Simpson, Christopher. *Blowback: America's Recruitment of Nazis and Its Effect on the Cold War*. London: Weidenfeld & Nicolson, 1988.

Steven, Stewart. *The Spymasters of Israel*. New York: Macmillan, 1980.

Tetens, T. H. *The New Germany and the Old Nazis*. London: Secker & Warburg, 1961.

*Thomas, Gordon. *Gideon's Spies: The Secret History of the Mossad*. New York: St. Martin's Press, 2000.

The Trial of Adolf Eichmann: Record of Proceedings in the District Court of Jerusalem. 9 vols. Jerusalem: Trust for the Publication of the Proceedings of the Eichmann Trial, 1992.

Tschuy, Theo. *Dangerous Diplomacy: The Story of Carl Lutz, Rescuer of 62,000 Hungarian Jews*. Grand Rapids, MI: William B. Eerdmans, 2000.

Von Lang, Jochen, ed. *Eichmann Interrogated*. New York: Farrar, Straus & Giroux, 1983.

Weber, Gaby. *La Conexion Alemana: El Lavado del Dinero Nazi en Argentina*. Buenos Aires: Edhasa, 2005.

*Wiesenthal, Simon. *Justice Not Vengeance*. New York: Grove-Weidenfeld, 1989.

Wiesenthal, Simon and Joseph Wechsberg, ed. *The Murderers Among Us: The Simon Wiesenthal Memoirs*. New York: McGraw-Hill, 1967.

Wighton, Charles. *Eichmann: His Career and Crimes*. London: Odhams Press, 1961.

Williams, Charles. *Adenauer: The Father of the New Germany*. Boston: Little, Brown, 2000.

Wojak, Irmtrud. *Eichmann Memoiren: Ein Kritischer Essay*. Frankfurt: Campus Verlag, 2001.

*Yablonka, Hanna. *The State of Israel vs. Adolf Eichmann*. New York: Schocken Books, 2004.

Yahil, Leni. *The Holocaust: The Fate of European Jewry, 1932–1945*. New York: Oxford University Press, 1990.

Zweig, Ronald W. *The Gold Train: The Destruction of Jews and the Looting of Hungary*. New York: HarperCollins, 2002.

Notes

In citing works in the notes, short titles have generally been used. Works frequently cited have been identified by the following abbreviations.

AdsD-Archiv der Sozialen Demokratie der Friedrich Ebert Stiftung, Bonn
AGN-Archivo General de la Nación, Buenos Aires
BArch-Bundesarchiv, Koblenz
CZA-Central Zionist Archives, Jerusalem
HAE-The Hunt for Adolf Eichmann
IMAE-I Met Adolf Eichmann
ISA-Israel State Archives, Jerusalem
NA-National Archives, Washington, DC
YVS-Yad Vashem, Jerusalem

Epigraph
"I sat at my desk": Lauryssens, p. 77.
"We will bring Adolf Eichmann": Malkin, *Eichmann in My Hands*, pp. 140–4.

Chapter 1
Lieutenant Colonel Adolf Eichmann stood: "Eichmann Memoirs," p. 23; Aschenauer, pp. 332–33.
He held his trim frame stiff: Boyle, p. 5; NA, RG 319, IRR, Adolf Eichmann, "Interrogation of Dieter Wisliceny," December 2, 1946.
He ran his office: Cesarani, pp. 117–58.
Stage one was: Zweig, pp. 49–59.
To prevent escapes: Cesarani, pp. 162–69; Braham, pp. 434–37; Aschenauer, p. 336.
At dawn: YVS, O.3, File 6151, Testimony of Zeev Sapir, April 9, 1990; Z. Sapir interview, *IMAE*; Braham, pp. 590–94; Mermelstein, pp. 2, 74.
"Jews: You have": YVS, Testimony of Zeev Sapir; Z. Sapir interview, *IMAE*. In his account, Sapir also details how Eichmann executed several ghetto prisoners, but since there is no corroboration of this occurrence in any other historical record, I have excluded the event. That said, it is clear from other histories that Eichmann was indeed touring Carpatho-Ruthenia at this time and that these visits were recorded in the press. See Braham, pp. 606–7; Hausner, p. 139.
Soon after Eichmann's visit: YVS, Testimony of Zeev Sapir; Z. Sapir interview,

IMAE; Levai, *Eichmann in Hungary*, pp. 104–7; Nagy-Talavera, p. 289; Lengyel, pp. 6–23.

Four days after: YVS, Testimony of Zeev Sapir; Levi, pp. 18–19.

Adolf Eichmann had not: Erez.

Born in an industrial: Cesarani, pp. 1–156. In this biographical summary of Adolf Eichmann before Hungary, I have drawn heavily on the thorough and balanced biography by David Cesarani, *Becoming Eichmann*. Much of the Eichmann historiography paints him as either a deluded madman who was bent on the destruction of the Jews from cradle to grave or, thanks to Hannah Arendt, a sober, passionless desk clerk. Cesarani revealed a more realistic portrait. I also referenced the following sources in completing this summary: "Eichmann Memoirs"; BArch, Sassen Transcripts, 6/110; *The Trial of Adolf Eichmann*; Lawson; Reynolds; Von Lang, *Eichmann Interrogated*; Bukey; Wighton; Clarke; Yahil; Mulisch; Arendt; Mendelsohn and Detweiler, vol. 8, pp. 71–93. Any quotes have separate notes.

"The Führer has ordered": Von Lang, *Eichmann Interrogated*, p. 81.

Eichmann was sent: Ibid., pp. 74–77.

"given their orders": *The Trial of Adolf Eichmann*, p. 1423.

"They were stealing": "Eichmann Memoirs," p. 14.

While away from: Cesarani, pp. 186–88; NA, RG 319, IRR, Eichmann, "Interrogation of Dieter Wisliceny"; *The Trial of Adolf Eichmann*, pp. 1789, 1834, 1855, 1971; Levai, *Black Book*, p. 109.

"You see, I'm back": Yahil, p. 517.

There were no trains: Yahil, pp. 152–53; Levai, *Eichmann in Hungary*, pp. 14, 164–66; Braham, pp. 834–43.

"If until now": *The Trial of Adolf Eichmann*, p. 1530.

When Zeev Sapir arrived: YVS, Testimony of Zeev Sapir; Z. Sapir interview, *IMAE*; *The Trial of Adolf Eichmann*, pp. 970–74; Muller, pp. 135–38; Lengyel, pp. 16–20.

Then it was winter: *The Trial of Adolf Eichmann*, pp. 970–74; YVS, Testimony of Zeev Sapir; Z. Sapir interview, *IMAE*; Gutman and Berenbaum, pp. 50–57.

They trudged through: YVS, Testimony of Zeev Sapir; Z. Sapir interview, *IMAE*; *The Trial of Adolf Eichmann*, pp. 970–74.

"I will gladly": "Eichmann Memoirs," p. 46; *The Trial of Adolf Eichmann*, p. 1804.

The village was teeming: Höttl, pp. 301–2; Black, pp. 234–37.

Then he went: Lawson; Aschenauer, p. 423.

Chapter 2

"Have you heard": Wiesenthal, *The Murderers Among Us*, p. 100.

Only four weeks earlier: Ibid., pp. 10–14; Pick, pp. 31–98.

The name Eichmann: Wiesenthal, *The Murderers Among Us*, p. 100.

"Eichmann!": Wiesenthal, *Justice Not Vengeance*, p. 67.

On July 28: NA, RG 319, IRR, Adolf Eichmann, "Summary of Interrogation Reports from Counter Intelligence War Room, London," November 19, 1945; Wiesenthal, *The Murderers Among Us*, p. 101.

Handsome as a movie star: Diamant; Ben-Natan, pp. 72–74.

"Thank you": Diamant; Briggs, p. 164.

Hundreds of copies: NA, RG 319, IRR, Adolf Eichmann, CIC Report on Adolf Eichmann, June 7, 1947.

That December: Friedman, *The Hunter*, pp. 176–85.

"There are some people": CZA, Z 6/842, Letter from Simon Wiesenthal to Nahum Goldmann, March 30, 1954; Wiesenthal, *The Murderers Among Us*, p. 123.

Upon his return: Pick, pp. 131–35; Wiesenthal, *The Murderers Among Us*, p. 124; Levy, pp. 123–24.

Soon after: Wiesenthal, *The Murderers Amongst Us*, p. 124.

His disappointment at failing: Wiesenthal, *Justice Not Vengeance*, p. 74.

"It would have been": Harel, p. 17.

His dinner guest: A. Hahn, author interview; A. Kleinert, author interview.

He had to alert: AdsD, Nachlass Fritz Bauer, Box 1, Letter from Lothar Hermann to Fritz Bauer, June 25, 1960.

A few weeks later: A. Hahn, author interview; A. Kleinert, author interview; Friedman, *The Blind Man*; Harel, pp. 18–19. To recount the scene of Sylvia Hermann's visit to the Eichmann house, I drew on these four primary sources, which contradict one another on various levels. What is beyond doubt is that Hermann found the address of Adolf Eichmann and presented herself at the house to see if Nick's father was indeed the Nazi war criminal, an act of tremendous courage.

Chapter 3

Near the crystal-blue: A. Shalom, author interview; Y. Gat, author interview; Bar-Zohar, *Spies in the Promised Land*, p. 156; Bar-Zohar, *The Avengers*, p. 161.

Harel was the youngest: Bar-Zohar, *Spies in the Promised Land*, pp. 3–40; Black and Benny, pp. 25–47; Steven, pp. 36–46.

In 1947: Deacon, p. 56.

"Abdullah is going": Derogy and Carmel, pp. 84–85.

Two months later: Steven, pp. 15–16.

Now, on a late September: Harel, pp. 1–2.

The Mossad's lack: Fried, pp. 1–4; Douglas, pp. 154–56; Yablonka, p. 12.

Harel himself was haunted: Harel, pp. 2–3.

He read transcripts: Diamant; Bower, p. 393.

Harel was completely: Harel, pp. 2–3.

Harel wanted to know: Ibid., pp. 4–9.

In January 1958: Harel, pp. 10–12; Aharoni, *On Life and Death*, p. 117.

Harel had tremendous: ISA, 3037/2-a, Biography of Hofstetter, March 21, 1961.

Hofstetter arrived in Buenos Aires: Harel, pp. 14–15.

He was greeted: Documentary Interview Notes, *HAE*; Y. Gat, author interview; L. Volk, author interview.

After some inquiries: A. Kleinert, author interview.

"My name is": Harel, pp. 16–22; AdsD, Nachlass Fritz Bauer, Box 1, Letter from Lothar Hermann to Fritz Bauer, June 25, 1960.

On April 8: Harel, pp. 24–26; AdsD, Nachlass Fritz Bauer, Box 1, Letter from Lothar Hermann to Fritz Bauer, June 25, 1960; ISA, 6384/4-g, Letter from Lothar Hermann to Tuviah Friedman, June 5, 1960.

His letter wound: Harel, pp. 26–27.

At the end of August: Harel, p. 27.

The trail went cold: Aharoni, *On Life and Death*, pp. 117–22; Y. Gat, author interview. Although Isser Harel claimed in his autobiography that he never lost interest in the Bauer tip, it is clear from the evidence and the testimony of agents who later participated in the operation to capture Eichmann in 1960 that Harel did indeed shelve the dossier.

Chapter 4

This was information: Despite many efforts in Germany and Israel to uncover this source, I was unable to prove any of the abundant theories on his or her identity. One candidate was Willem Sassen, a Dutch journalist who had served in the SS's corps of propagandists and later moved to Buenos Aires. On numerous occasions, he interviewed Adolf Eichmann in the development of a never-published memoir he wanted to cowrite with Sassen that would "counter the enemy propaganda" about Eichmann's activities during the war. Stan Lauryssens, the author of a biography on Sassen, presents the idea that Sassen was the informant (based largely on the confirmed fact that Sassen later worked with the Mossad on finding Mengele). See Lauryssens. Others state that the information came from captured Nazi smugglers in Austria or a fugitive Nazi who wanted to get back at Eichmann for past wrongs. See Derogy and Carmel; Hausner. I suspect that the information came from an agent in the German intelligence services (likely from a fugitive Nazi in Argentina), particularly given the continued silence on the subject.

Zvi Aharoni and Isser Harel: Z. Aharoni interview, *IMAE*; Aharoni, *On Life and Death*, pp. 121–25; Producer's Notes, *HAE*.

"This is simply unbelievable": Aharoni, *On Life and Death*, p. 123.

"I want Zvi": Ibid., p. 125.

Harel agreed: Z. Aharoni interview, *IMAE*; Harel, pp. 32–37.

Though equal in height: Bar-Zohar, *Spies in the Promised Land*, p. 110.

Haim Cohen joined them: Harel, p. 37.

"Prevent Bauer": Derogy and Carmel, p. 177.

Harel knew this type: Shpiro, *Geheimdienste in der Weltgeschichte*.

But Ben-Gurion was clear: Wojak, p. 40; Yablonka, pp. 46–47; Harel, p. 38.

"Isser will deal": Bar-Zohar, *Ben-Gurion*, p. 1374.

Three weeks later: NA, RG 263, Nazis/West Germany/Post WWII, *Current Intelligence Weekly Summary*, February 18, 1960; Williams, p. 478.

"evoked pictures": Tetens, p. 149.

West German Chancellor: NA, RG 263, Nazis/West Germany/Post WWII, *Current Intelligence Weekly Summary*, February 18, 1960; *Time*, January 20, 1960; Fulbrook, p. 63; Tetens, pp. 42–60; Prittie, pp. 278–81.

"almost nationwide": Tetens, p. 222; NA, RG 263, Nazis/West Germany/Post WWII, CIA Report, "Growth of Neo-Nazism," March 21, 1958.

Soon after the Cologne: Producer's Notes, *HAE*.

Chapter 5

His Israeli diplomatic papers: Documentary Transcript, *HAE*.

Aharoni had the kind: Aharoni, *On Life and Death*, pp. 9–102.

Aharoni was met: Z. Aharoni interview, *IMAE*; Aharoni and Dietl, pp. 88–91.

Two days later: Z. Aharoni interview, *IMAE*; Harel, pp. 43–45.

Roberto was one: Thomas, p. 68.

"For my friend": Z. Aharoni interview, *IMAE*.

"Excuse me, please": Aharoni and Dietl, pp. 92–96.

Listening to Juan's: Documentary Interview Notes, *HAE*; Harel, pp. 48–51.

Confident in what: Aharoni and Dietl, pp. 88, 97.

On March 8: Ibid., p. 97.

Aharoni started the car: Harel, pp. 98–103.

"Go back tomorrow": Research Notes, *HAE*.

On March 12: Aharoni and Dietl, pp. 103–4.

"And what do you": Ibid.; Harel, pp. 59–60.

Later that afternoon: Documentary Interview Notes, *HAE*.

"What happened": Research Notes, *HAE*.

"Ah. Never mind": Z. Aharoni interview, *IMAE*.

The next day: Aharoni and Dietl, pp. 106–7.

He spotted a one-story: *La Razon*, April 24, 1961; *Ahora*, June 7, 1960; Lauryssens, p. 117.

Aharoni noticed: Z. Aharoni interview, *IMAE*.

On March 16: Z. Aharoni interview, *IMAE*; Aharoni and Dietl, pp. 106–12.

"It's possible there's been": Research Notes, *HAE*.

Chapter 6

Over the past: Harel, p. 76; Demo Tape, *HAE*; Thomas, p. 75; Bar-Zohar, *Spies in the Promised Land*, pp. 108–9; Rein, pp. 143, 157–59.

Zvi Aharoni lay: Aharoni and Dietl, pp. 116–18.

Vardi was an Israeli: Ben-Natan, pp. 84, 90.

Vardi understood: Aharoni and Dietl, pp. 118–19.

On Sunday, April 3: Z. Aharoni interview, *IMAE*; Harel, pp. 73–77.

"Are you definitively sure": Research Notes, *HAE*.

Chapter 7

In February 1945: Meding, p. 50.

"It's a mere": Newton, p. xv; Meding, p. 50.

He wanted Nazi: Rathkolb, pp. 205–20.

The Argentine secret service: Meding, pp. 46–54; Goñi, pp. 101–15. No author can discuss the movement of war criminals to Argentina without referencing Uki Goñi's *The Real Odessa* and Holger Meding's *Flücht vor Nürnberg?* In particular when it comes to Adolf Eichmann, Goñi provides incredible insight into the machinations by which he entered Argentina.

Argentina was not alone: NA, RG 59, 800.0128/5-1547, "La Vista Report"; Simpson, pp. 185–87; Breitman, pp. 350–420.

Munich was swarming: Aarons and Loftus, p. 40.

On May 31: Eichmann Immigration Card, Direccion Nacional de Migraciones (DNM), Buenos Aires; *Giovanna C* Passenger List, July 1950, DNM; Goñi, pp. 292–317; Eichmann, *Meine Flucht*.

Eichmann had 485 pesos: Eichmann, *Meine Flucht*; AGN, Martin Bormann File; AGN, Josef Mengele File.

"the uncle of": Aharoni and Dietl, p. 67.

When Vera and the boys: "Interview with Klaus Eichmann"; Lawson; Lauryssens, p. 39.

"Veronika": Lawson.

On April 10: A. Shalom, author interview.

Now he was the Deputy: A. Shalom, author interview.

"How would you feel": A. Shalom, author interview.

The first choice: A. Shalom, author interview; Y. Gat, author interview; Demo Tape, *HAE*.

The Mossad staff: Steven, p. 111; A. Shalom, author interview.

Any equipment: A. Shalom, author interview; Malkin, *Eichmann in My Hands*, p. 128.

As the Israeli: Yablonka, p. 46; Papadatos, pp. 52–62; Robinson, pp. 103–6.

Over the next: Harel, p. 89; *New York Times*, March 16, 1960.

Each night: Malkin, *Eichmann in My Hands*, p. 127.

He had already contacted: Harel, pp. 38–39.

"Okay, everyone": Malkin, *Eichmann in My Hands*, p. 140.

"I want to begin": Demo Tape, *HAE*.

"We will bring": Malkin, *Eichmann in My Hands*, pp. 140–41.

Chapter 8

On April 24: Y. Gat, author interview; Harel, pp. 102–3.

He had flown to Rome: A. Shalom, author interview.

"Compatriot": Ibid.

"What do you want": Ibid.; Y. Gat, author interview.

Early the next morning: Y. Gat, author interview.

He had already: Harel, pp. 86–89, 99–100.

"Look, friends": B. Tirosh, author interview.

Peleg was noticeably: Harel, p. 109.

Harel stressed that: B. Tirosh, author interview.

"Will you be able": S. Shaul, author interview.

"It is a very": B. Tirosh, author interview.

Lying flat: A. Shalom, author interview; Y. Gat, author interview; Aharoni and Dietl, pp. 128–29.

They needed to find: A. Shalom, author interview; Documentary Interview Notes, *HAE*.

In the best case: A. Shalom, author interview; J. Moskoviz, author interview.

"The initial team": Harel, p. 111.

"Dead or alive": Bar-Zohar, *Ben Gurion*, p. 1375; Derogy and Carmel, p. 176.

Chapter 9

Shalom and Gat spent: A. Shalom, author interview.

Their own cars: Yaakov Medad interview, Massuah Institute; Documentary Interview Notes, *HAE*; A. Shalom, author interview.

Yosef Klein, the manager: Y. Klein, author interview.

Shimoni shifted in his seat: Y. Klein, author interview.

For a while: Y. Klein, author interview; Harel, pp. 123–25.

"What your job": Y. Klein, author interview.

On May 3: Harel, p. 135.

The first was in: Malkin, *Eichmann in My Hands*, p. 168; A. Shalom, author interview.

This second and better: Malkin, *The Argentina Journal*, p. 48; Harel, p. 132.

After the El Al: A. Shalom, author interview; Harel, p. 130.

On the evening: Malkin, *Eichmann in My Hands*, pp. 153–56.

His hands numb: Peter Malkin interview, Steven Spielberg Jewish Film Archive; Malkin, *Eichmann in My Hands*, pp. 155–56.

What none of: Aharoni and Dietl, pp. 130–31; Z. Aharoni interview, *IMAE*; Documentary Interview Notes, *HAE*.

Chapter 10

At Ezeiza Airport: Y. Klein, author interview; Harel, p. 138.

Back at Maoz: Malkin, *Eichmann in My Hands*, pp. 163–64; Harel, pp. 136–37.

Meanwhile, Avraham Shalom: A. Shalom, author interview; Harel, p. 148.

He also assisted: Yaakov Medad interview, Massuah Institute; Aharoni and Dietl, p. 132.

Throughout all this: Peter Malkin interview, Steven Spielberg Jewish Film Archive; Malkin, *Eichmann in My Hands*, p. 132.

On May 8: Harel, pp. 142–43.

"We're glad you're here": Malkin, *Eichmann in My Hands*, pp. 169–70.

A hand-drawn map: Malkin, *Eichmann in My Hands*, p. 143.

The Chevrolet would be: Harel, p. 147; Aharoni and Dietl, pp. 133–34; A. Shalom, author interview; M. Tabor interview, *IMAE*; P. Malkin interview, *HAE*.

On May 9: R. Eitan, author interview.

He sat down with: Harel, pp. 147–49.

"We're planning": Y. Klein, author interview.

Klein had mapped: Ibid.

Now Klein told: Ibid.; Harel, pp. 152–53.

At Tira: M. Tabor interview, *IMAE*; Producer's Notes, *HAE*; Malkin, *Eichmann in My Hands*, pp. 168–69.

"Can you tell me": Aharoni and Dietl, p. 138.

Meanwhile, in the garage: A. Shalom, author interview.

"You were chosen": Harel, p. 150.

What should they do: Aharoni and Dietl, p. 183.

What would happen: Ibid., p. 136; A. Shalom, author interview.

What if they: Harel, p. 150.

As many of the team: R. Eitan, author interview.

"Are there any questions": Y. Gat, author interview.

Chapter 11

When the Mossad team: Malkin, *Eichmann in My Hands*, pp. 181–83.

Adolf Eichmann began: Lawson; Pearlman, p. 1.

This bus was filled: "Eichmann File," Tribunales Federales de Comodoro Py, Buenos Aires.

At the plant: Ibid.; *Clarin*, May 27, 1960; Pearlman, p. 4.

Zvi Aharoni turned: Malkin, *Eichmann in My Hands*, p. 184; P. Malkin interview, Steven Spielberg Jewish Film Archive.

Gat was in the: Y. Gat, author interview.

In five minutes: A. Shalom, author interview.

Aharoni stopped: Aharoni and Dietl, pp. 136–37; M. Tabor interview, *IMAE*.

"Thank you": Aharoni and Dietl, p. 137; Malkin, *The Argentina Journal*, p. 102.

Malkin prepared himself: P. Malkin interview, Steven Spielberg Jewish Film Archive; P. Malkin interview, *HAE*; M. Tabor interview, *IMAE*; Pearlman, p. 53.

They had no guns: A. Shalom, author interview.

The lights from the bus: Harel, p. 162; Z. Aharoni interview, *IMAE*.

Malkin looked toward: P. Malkin interview, Steven Spielberg Jewish Film Archive; P. Malkin interview, *HAE*; McKechnie and Howell.

Shalom and Gat: A. Shalom, author interview; Y. Gat, author interview.

"Do we take off": R. Eitan, author interview.

Tabor and Malkin: M. Tabor interview, *IMAE*.

At 8:05 P.M.: A. Shalom, author interview; P. Malkin interview, *HAE*; P. Malkin interview, Steven Spielberg Jewish Film Archive; Research Notes, *HAE*; M. Tabor interview, *IMAE*; Y. Gat, author interview; R. Eitan, author interview; Aharoni and Dietl, pp. 136–39; Harel, pp. 163–65; Malkin, *Eichmann in My Hands*, pp. 185–87.

Isser Harel sat alone: Harel, pp. 160–61.

There was no way: Demo Tape, *HAE*; A. Shalom, author interview.

He stared at: Harel, p. 161.

Chapter 12

Eichmann staggered uneasily: M. Tabor interview, *IMAE*; Peter Malkin interview, Steven Spielberg Jewish Film Archive; Malkin, *The Argentina Journal*, p. 105.

Eichmann stood: Malkin, *Eichmann in My Hands*, p. 188.

Aharoni could not fathom: Aharoni and Dietl, p. 140.

"No man can": NA, RG 263, Adolf Eichmann Name File (CIA), General Expansiveness of [excised], August 24, 1961.

He found several: P. Malkin interview, Steven Spielberg Jewish Film Archive.

This was the moment: Aharoni, *On Life and Death*, pp. 98–101.

"What's your name": Aharoni and Dietl, pp. 142–43; Harel, pp. 166–67; Z. Aharoni interview, *IMAE*; Research Notes, *HAE*; P. Malkin interview, Steven Spielberg Jewish Film Archive; A. Shalom, author interview; Friedman, *The Blind Man*. The exact transcript of the interrogation is not available. Aharoni and Harel recounted their versions as definitive. I have drawn from these two as well as the recollections of several others.

Joy erupted in the room: A. Shalom, author interview; Y. Gat, author interview.

They drove into: A. Shalom, author interview; Aharoni and Dietl, pp. 143–44; Y. Medad interview, Massuah Institute.

When they reached: Harel, p. 161.

As Shalom gave: A. Shalom, author interview; Aharoni and Dietl, pp. 143–44.

"The typewriter": Documentary Interview Notes, *HAE*.

"That's all": Harel, pp. 169–70.

Back on Garibaldi Street: Lawson; Lauryssens, p. 125.

"I'm going back": Malkin, *Eichmann in My Hands*, p. 192.

Hours later: Malkin, *The Argentina Journal*, p. 74.

This was only: A. Shalom, author interview; Y. Gat, author interview; Aharoni and Dietl, p. 155.

Tabor had already: M. Tabor interview, *IMAE*.

He lay on the bed: Malkin, *Eichmann in My Hands*, p. 193.

After daybreak: Y. Gat, author interview; A. Shalom, author interview.

"I just have": Malkin, *Eichmann in My Hands*, p. 194.

"Why did you": Harel, p. 190.

"Why didn't your family": Z. Aharoni interview, *IMAE*.

"Are you prepared": Z. Aharoni interview, *IMAE*.

Chapter 13

"The old man is gone": "Interview with Klaus Eichmann."

They went to see: Ibid.; AGN, Martin Bormann File. In Klaus Eichmann's recollection of this day recounted to *Quick* magazine, he stated only that he went to his father's "best friend," not Carlos Fuldner. However, the Argentine archives reveal in a police report/interview with Fuldner that the Eichmann sons came to him, although he said that this occurred only after it was reported publicly that Eichmann had been taken by the Israelis. This later date seems suspect, and it is my conclusion that Fuldner and the "best friend" were the same individual.

Vera Eichmann went: "Eichmann File," Tribunales Federales de Comodoro Py, Buenos Aires; Weber, pp. 135–39.

Then a search around: Anderson, p. 98.

Nick and Dieter pawned: "Interview with Klaus Eichmann."

Tacuara had been: Anonymous Tacuara members, author interview; Gutman; Marty.

Though not in Tacuara: "Interview with Klaus Eichmann"; Anonymous Tacuara members, author interview; Demo Tape, *HAE*; Gutman. In his interview with *Quick*, Klaus Eichmann referred to a "Peronist youth group" that came to their aid. It is clear from interviews with several Tacuara members, as well as from the research of Marty and Gutman, that this group was in fact Tacuara.

"Are you the man": P. Malkin interview, Steven Spielberg Jewish Film Archive; P. Malkin interview, *HAE*; Malkin, *Eichmann in My Hands*, pp. 201–4. There have been some arguments about whether it was possible for Malkin to carry on these conversations. In his memoir, Isser Harel related how Malkin spoke to Eichmann at length, but Aharoni discounted that possibility because of the lack of a common language. Other operatives on the mission have said that Malkin did speak to Eichmann. Further, Malkin's recollections of these conversations are pretty consistent, both in his memoir and in the interviews cited above. I have attempted to relate only those conversations that I have confirmed in both his book and the interviews, although they required some spare editing to make sense to readers.

Too scared to attempt: P. Malkin interview, Steven Spielberg Jewish Film Archive.

The day after: Y. Klein, author interview.

Using Klein's information: Y. Klein, author interview; M. Tabor interview, *IMAE*; Aharoni and Dietl, pp. 156–60.

"Stop insulting me": Aharoni and Dietl, p. 152.

When he had met: Harel, pp. 194–98; Z. Aharoni interview, *IMAE*.

"The sight of": Harel, p. 184.

"I know what": Malkin, *Eichmann in My Hands*, p. 236.

By May 17: A. Shalom, author interview; Y. Gat, author interview; Harel, pp. 194–98.

A few tasks: M. Tabor interview, *IMAE*; Aharoni and Dietl, pp. 157–58.

"To even be": Malkin, *Eichmann in My Hands*, p. 223.

Chapter 14

On a clear: Eban, pp. 306–13; Kurzman, p. 424.

Every effort at secrecy: Harel, pp. 221–26; S. Alony, author interview; D. Alon, author interview; "Eichmann File," Tribunales Federales de Comodoro Py, Buenos Aires.

"Announcing the departure": Reynolds, p. 9.

At exactly: S. Shaul, author interview.

That night: "Interview with Klaus Eichmann"; Anonymous Tacuara members, author interview; S. Sassen, author interview; A. Levavi, author interview.

"Don't do anything stupid": "Interview with Klaus Eichmann."

"Let me ask you this": Malkin, *Eichmann in My Hands*, p. 218.

"You do realize": Ibid.

Eichmann showed no emotion: Ibid., p. 220.

The prisoner drained his glass: P. Malkin interview, Steven Spielberg Jewish Film Archive; Harel, pp. 208–9; Y. Gat, author interview; Y. Medad interview, Massuah Institute; Aharoni and Dietl, pp. 152–53. The signing of the statement by Eichmann is rife with conflicting stories. In Aharoni's memoir, he stated that he was the one who prompted Eichmann to sign, an assertion that has been supported by Avraham Shalom and Yaakov Gat. Meanwhile, Malkin, backed by Isser Harel's account, stated that he secured the signature. Given that Harel had access to all of the postoperation accounts, I chose to present the Malkin version, although I accept the possibility that it was a more collaborative process. In fact, this is how Rafi Eitan remembers the signing unfolding.

"I, the undersigned": ISA, 2150/4-hz, Letter from Michael Comay, Israeli UN representative, to President of UN Security Council, June 21, 1960.

"What date should": Hausner, p. 275.

"What the hell": Malkin, *Eichmann in My Hands*, p. 232; Y. Medad interview, Massuah Institute.

Shmuel Wedeles pointed: Collective testimony from El Al flight crew, author interview.

Ten minutes later: B. Tirosh, author interview; S. Shaul, author interview; D. Alon, author interview.

Shortly after the plane's: Harel, pp. 230–31.

He gathered: A. Shalom, author interview; D. Alon, author interview.

Chapter 15

At Maoz, Shalom Dani: Harel, pp. 243–44.

Moshe Tabor spent: M. Tabor interview, *IMAE*; R. Eitan, author interview.

Avraham Shalom was also: A. Shalom, author interview.

At the safe house: Y. Gat, author interview; Malkin, *Eichmann in My Hands*, pp. 240–41.

"It isn't necessary": Malkin, *Eichmann in My Hands*, pp. 241–43; Aharoni and

Dietl, p. 163; A. Shalom, author interview; Y. Gat, author interview; R. Eitan, author interview.

"We're advancing": S. Shabtai, author interview; D. Alon, author interview; D. Sasson, author interview.

Aharoni took a long: Aharoni and Dietl, p. 164; Y. Gat, author interview.

In the parking lot: Harel, pp. 250–51.

"Be absolutely silent": Y. Gat, author interview.

"Form a circle": D. Alon, author interview.

"Pretend to sleep": D. Alon, author interview; S. Shabtai, author interview; D. Sasson, author interview.

In the terminal restaurant: Harel, pp. 254–55.

Harel left his: A. Shalom, author interview.

"You surprise me": Y. Klein, author interview.

As midnight approached: Aharoni and Dietl, p. 165.

As Harel boarded: Harel, p. 255.

"El Al is ready": S. Shaul, author interview; B. Tirosh, author interview; O. Kabiri, author interview.

Chapter 16

Yosef Klein paced: Y. Klein, author interview.

"What is the problem": S. Shaul, author interview.

Once they had crossed: S. Shabtai, author interview.

"You've been accorded": Harel, p. 260.

Zvi Tohar: O. Kabiri, author interview; S. Shaul, author interview; D. Alon, author interview.

Hour after hour: S. Shaul, author interview; Harel, pp. 260–66.

The morning after: Y. Klein, author interview.

The final task: A. Shalom, author interview; R. Eitan, author interview.

In the Britannia: D. Sasson, author interview; D. Alon, author interview; O. Kabiri, author interview; S. Shaul, author interview; Y. Gat, author interview.

Isser Harel congratulated: Harel, pp. 268–69.

Elian injected Eichmann: Y. Gat, author interview.

The rest of the stopover: A. Shalom, author interview.

They had already: S. Shaul, author interview.

The plane flew up: Ibid.; D. Alon, author interview.

When the plane: Harel, p. 269.

Chapter 17

At 6:55 A.M.: Aharoni and Dietl, p. 116.

There was no celebration: S. Shabtai, author interview.

The captain also: S. Shaul, author interview.

"The monster is": B. Tirosh, author interview.

Tabor and Gat escorted: Y. Gat, author interview; Reynolds, pp. 10–11.

"I brought you": Harel, p. 271; Bar-Zohar, *Ben Gurion*, pp. 1374–77.

A few hours later: ISA, 3039/1-a, Hofstetter Memo; Harel, p. 274.

"How many people": R. Eitan, author interview.

"I am Adolf Eichmann": Yablonka, p. 31. Curiously, Halevi issued the warrant under the International Treaty for the Convention on the Prevention and Punishment of the Crime of Genocide (under the UN charter), which applied only to crimes committed after 1949. The correct law would have been Israel's Nazi and Nazi Collaborators Law (1950).

In a restaurant: AdsD, Nachlass Fritz Bauer, Box 1, Letter from Haim Cohen to Dr. Fritz Bauer, May 22, 1960; Harel, pp. 274–75.

"I have to inform": "The Beast in Chains," *Time*, June 6, 1960; Robinson, p. 105.

"When they had": Robinson, p. 106.

On May 25: A. Shalom, author interview.

Shalom discovered that: Ibid.; Y. Gat, author interview.

"You were in": M. Tabor interview, *IMAE*.

"Look, didn't you": Malkin, *Eichmann in My Hands*, p. 250.

"I'm not naive": Aharoni and Dietl, p. 167.

Chapter 18

Outside Haifa: Von Lang, *Eichmann Interrogated*, pp. xix–xx; S. Nagar interview, *IMAE*.

In Israel, the shock: Yablonka, p. 36.

"The Jewish state": Cesarani, p. 239.

As for the half: Yablonka, pp. 36–37.

"Israeli agents": *Time*, June 1, 1960.

"Jewish volunteers": ISA, 2150/4-hz, Letter from the Permanent Representative of Israel to the President of the Security Council, June 21, 1960.

Unable to strike: Rein, pp. 206–7; Haim.

By the fall: "Eichmann File," Tribunales Federales de Comodoro Py, Buenos Aires.

In the valley: Musmanno, pp. 11–13; Arendt, p. 3.

"Adolf Eichmann, rise": Guri, p. 2.

"First count": *The Trial of Adolf Eichmann*, pp. 3–10.

"When I stand": Ibid., p. 62.

Once Hausner finished: Cesarani, pp. 272–74.

Given his clipped: Mulisch, p. 127.

He was unmoved: Cesarani, pp. 272, 282–305. The Israeli court allowed only a small portion of the Sassen documents to be entered into evidence — just those pages that Eichmann had handwritten or to which he had added comments while editing his memoirs in Argentina.

"For the dispatch": *The Trial of Adolf Eichmann*, p. 2218.

Eichmann stood absolutely still: Guri, p. 299.

"I hope, very much": Malkin, *Eichmann in My Hands*, p. 173.

"Long live Germany": Hull, p. 159; Arye Wallenstein, "Eichmann Dies on the Gallows," Reuters, June 1, 1962.

The two guards hit: Hull, pp. 160–69; M. Gilead interview, *IMAE*; Hausner, p. 446.

Epilogue

David Ben-Gurion achieved: Yablonka, pp. 250–51.

In the rest: Cesarani, pp. 324–57.

Now a professor: Ricardo Eichmann, letter to author, December 2006.

Of the three: Aharoni and Dietl, pp. 176-77.

In the weeks after: NA, RG 263, Nazis/West Germany/Post WWII, Current Intelligence Weekly Summary, July 7, 1960; Cesarani, p. 335.

Simon Wiesenthal won: "The Eichmann Chase"; Pick, pp. 151–327.

"She can't talk": Malkin, *Eichmann in My Hands*, p. 258; P. Malkin interview, Steven Spielberg Jewish Film Archive.

Photo credits

Front cover, top: © Roger Viollet/The Image Works; front cover, knife: Sergii Denysov/iStockphoto, Galina Ermolaeva/iStockphoto, Gabor Kecskemeti/iStockphoto; back cover: AP Images; i: Mossad Archives, Photograph by Elad Sarig/Courtesy Beit Hatfutsot, The Museum of the Jewish People; ii–iii: Estate of Zvi Aharoni, Courtesy Wilhelm Dietl Collection; 4: AP Images; 7: Ghetto Fighters House Museum/Courtesy United States Holocaust Memorial Museum Photo Archives; 8: Yad Vashem; 10: Yad Vashem; 12: © Roger Viollet/The Image Works; 14: Popperfoto/Getty Images; 17: Yad Vashem; 22: Gamma-Keystone via Getty Images; 24: Massuah Institute for Holocaust Studies, Kibbutz Tel Itzhak, Israel; 26: Yad Vashem; 29: Yad Vashem; 31: Robert Lackenbach/Time & Life Pictures/Getty Images; 33: Yad Vashem; 35: Mossad Archives, Photograph by Elad Sarig/Courtesy Beit Hatfutsot, The Museum of the Jewish People; 38: Moshe Milner/State of Israel, Government Press Office photo collection; 47: Estate of Zvi Aharoni, Courtesy Wilhelm Dietl Collection; 52–53: Yad Vashem; 64–65: Estate of Zvi Aharoni, Courtesy Wilhelm Dietl Collection; 67: Yad Vashem; 70: Estate of Zvi Aharoni, Courtesy Wilhelm Dietl Collection; 73: Estate of Zvi Aharoni, Courtesy Wilhelm Dietl Collection; 78: © Natacha Pisarenko/AP Photo; 80: Yad Vashem; 84: Mossad and Shin Bet Archives/Courtesy Beit Hatfutsot, The Museum of the Jewish People; 85: Mossad and Shin Bet Archives/Courtesy Beit Hatfutsot, The Museum of the Jewish People; 96: El Al Heritage Archive, Courtesy Marvin G. Goldman Collection; 100: Bettmann/Corbis; 102: El Al Heritage Archive, Courtesy Marvin G. Goldman Collection; 108–109: Mossad Archives, Photograph by Elad Sarig/Courtesy Beit Hatfutsot, The Museum of the Jewish People; 113: Mossad Archives, Photograph by Elad Sarig/Courtesy Beit Hatfutsot, The Museum of the Jewish People; 114: Courtesy Beit Hatfutsot, The Museum of the Jewish People; 122: Eddie Gerald/Demotix/Corbis; 133: Mossad Archives, Photograph by Elad Sarig/Courtesy Beit Hatfutsot, The Museum of the Jewish People; 136: Mossad Archives, Photograph by Elad Sarig/Courtesy Beit Hatfutsot, The Museum of the Jewish People; 143: Estate of Zvi Aharoni, Courtesy Wilhelm Dietl Collection; 147: Yad Vashem; 153: Mossad Archives, Photograph by Elad Sarig/Courtesy Beit Hatfutsot, The Museum of the Jewish People; 155: Peter R. Keating photo, Collections of John Wegg and Marvin G. Goldman; 158–159: Peter Z. Malkin, from *The Argentina Journal*, published by Victor Weiss, VWFPublishing.com; 169: © Dan Balilty/AP Photo; 171: Mossad Archives, Photograph by Elad Sarig/Courtesy Beit Hatfutsot, The Museum of the Jewish People; 182–183: Courtesy

Index

A

Aerolíneas Argentinas, 111, 116–117,
167, 172

Aharoni, Zvi (capture operation agent),
47, 47 (picture), 54, 137
in capture operation, 47, 82, 83,
86–90, 92–94, 98–99, 117–118,
121–122, 129–134
identification of Eichmann by, 66, 67
(picture), 68, 73–74
interrogation of Eichmann by,
135–144, 151, 160–162, 197
meeting with Bauer in Israel, 46–48
surveillance of Eichmann 54–63,
63–66, 64–65 (picture), 69–74, 70
(picture), 73 (picture), 94–95,
98–99, 106–110
See also capture operation; capture
operation agents

Allies, 5, 10–11, 19, 26, 75, 76

anti-Semitism, 27–29, 50–53, 52–53
(picture), 75–76, 146–147, 147
(picture), 197, 213–214

Argentina
anti-Semitism in, 27–29, 75–76,
146–147, 147 (picture), 197,
213–214
German community in, 28–30, 40,
43, 62, 75, 78–79, 145–146, 196
reaction to Eichmann's capture in,
196–198
WWII and relations with Germany,
30, 75–76
See also Buenos Aires; Ezeiza Airport

B

Bauer, Fritz (Nazi hunter), 31, 31
(picture), 46–48, 213–214
communication with Hermann,
30–31, 33, 35 (pictures)
descriptions of Eichmann, 43, 44
Harel on claims about Eichmann
and, 39–40, 41, 46–48, 49
reaction to Eichmann's capture, 190

Ben-Gurion, David (first Prime
Minister of Israel), 48–49; 100
(picture), 210
on capture of Eichmann 48–50, 51,
68–69, 99–100, 140, 154, 188–189,
190–195
education as goal of Eichmann trial,
212–213
on Israel's creation, 37

Brazil, 97, 156, 162–165, 175, 180

Bristol Britannia 4X-AGD. *See* El Al
Bristol Britannia flights

C

camps. *See* concentration camps

capture operation, 1–2, 86–90,
104–106, 115–120, 121–123,
128–134
authorization of, 68–69, 86–87,
99–100
cars used for, 1–2, 72, 101, 112, 115,
121, 123–126, 128, 132, 139
confirming Eichmann's identity
after, 135–136, 136 (picture)
contingency plans for, 133, 142, 149
transporting Eichmann to Israel, 167
goals of, 68–69
risks of, 68–69, 87, 90, 99–100,
118–120, 152
surveillance of Eichmann 63–66,
64–65 (picture), 69–74, 73
(picture), 94–95, 98–99, 114
transporting Eichmann to Israel,
96–97, 103–104, 117, 149–150,
165–168, 170–176, 180, 184–185,
188

capture operation agents
arrival in Buenos Aires, 91–94, 104,
106
choosing and selecting, 82–83
disgust of Eichmann by, 139, 144,
148, 149, 151–153, 157–161
forged documents for, 82, 84
(picture), 111–113, 133

capture operation agents (*continued*)
  individual responsibilities of, 117–118
  leaving Argentina after capture, 170, 181, 192, 193
  mood and activities during Eichmann's captivity, 151–153
  pictures of, 84–85
  sayanim used by, 54–63, 72–73, 140
  on silence and secrecy of mission, 193–195
Cohen, Haim, 46–50, 86–87, 144
Cologne, Germany, 50–52, 52 (picture), 190
Communism and Communists, 13, 28
concentration camps
  Auschwitz concentration camp, 9–10, 10 (picture), 14 (picture), 16–19, 103, 166, 199, 205
  Bergen-Belsen concentration camp, 112
  Dachau concentration camp, 29, 166
  Eichmann charged with crimes in, 199
  forced labor camps, 17 (picture)
  Gleiwitz concentration camp, 19
  Mauthausen concentration camp, 3, 21, 22
  as part of Hitler's Final Solution, 5
  See also Auschwitz concentration camp; Holocaust survivors
Coronel Suárez, Argentina, 30, 31, 41–42

D
Dani, Shalom (capture operation agent), 82, 84 (picture), 112
  forged documents made by, 93, 111–113, 152–153, 153 (picture), 167
  See also capture operation, capture operation agents
Diamant, Manus (Nazi hunter), 23–26, 24 (picture), 31
disguises 122, 165, 168–169

E
Eban, Abba, 154
Eichmann, Adolf Karl (Eichmann's father), 23, 199
Eichmann, Dieter "Dito" (Eichmann's son), 20, 25–26
  anti-Semitism of, 146–147, 156–157, 197, 213
  after father's capture, 145–147, 156–157, 197
  knowledge of Eichmann as father, 79
  surveillance of, 57–61, 70, 72

Eichmann, Horst (Eichmann's son), 20, 79
Eichmann, Klaus "Nick" (Eichmann's son), 20, 25–26, 79, 213
  anti-Semitism of, 28–30, 30, 146–147, 213
  after father's capture, 145–147, 156–157, 197
  relationship with Sylvia Hermann, 28–30, 32, 143
Eichmann, Ricardo (Eichmann's son), 213
Eichmann, Vera (Veronika) Leibl, 20, 24, 26 (picture), 79–81, 197, 213
  denial of Eichmann's war crimes by, 79, 81
  reaction to Eichmann missing, 140–141, 146
Eichmann (Adolf), in Argentina, 72 (picture), 75, 78–81, 80 (picture), 98, 122–123, 122 (picture), 146
  denial of guilt for war crimes by, 79, 81, 148–149, 157–161
  disguises and prep for El Al flight, 168–169
  family's search for after capture, 145–147, 156–157
  surveillance of 54–66, 64–65 (picture), 69–74, 73 (picture), 94–95, 98–99
Eichmann (Adolf), capture of, 1–2, 66 (picture), 122–123, 128–134, 141, 146
  assassination of *vs.*, 49–50
  confirming true identity of, 31–35, 42–45, 135–136, 136 (picture), 138–139, 189
  false identities of, 44–45, 48–50, 64–65 (picture), 66, 77–78, 78 (picture), 118–119, 122–123, 137–138, 143, 152–153, 153 (picture), 167, 171 (picture)
  interrogation and captivity of, 135–144, 143 (picture), 149, 151
  See also El Al Bristol Britannia flights; capture operation
Eichmann (Adolf), in Europe
  childhood and background of, 11–12
  escape from, 76–78, 78 (picture)
  hiding after end of war in, 19–20, 76
  Nazi/SS career in, 3–16, 4 (picture), 12 (picture), 22, 138
  Nazi hunters' search for, 23–28
Eichmann (Adolf), in Israel
  arrest and imprisonment of, 189–190, 191 (picture), 196–197

execution and cremation of, 208–210
last words of, 208–209
signed statement allowing for, 141,
  151, 160–162, 197
suicide precautions for, 196
Eichmann (Adolf), trial of,198–208
appeals and clemency requests, 205,
  208
guilty verdict and sentencing,
  204–207, 206–207 (picture)
importance of, 212
Israeli reaction to, 212–213, 212
  (picture)
Israel's right to prosecute, 87
Eitan, Rafi (capture operation agent),
  81, 84 (picture)
in capture operation, 82–83, 95–96,
  104, 106, 114–116, 119, 121–122,
  128–134, 141–142, 147–148, 162
as witness to Eichmann's execution,
  208
See also capture operation; capture
  operation agents
El Al Bristol Britannia flight (Buenos
  Aires to Tel Aviv)
Argentine Independence Day as
  cover for, 89, 146, 155
dates for, 105–106, 167
Eichmann on, 178, 181–182
final landing in Israel, 188
flight paths and refueling stops, 97,
  156, 163, 165–166, 175, 178–187,
  182–183 (picture), 186–187 (picture)
initial delay in take-off from
  Argentina, 177–178
prep and plans, 101–102, 149–150,
  155 (picture), 167–170, 177–178
transporting Eichmann to, 169–175
El Al Bristol Britannia flight (Tel Aviv
  to Buenos Aires), 96–97, 154, 156,
  162–166
El Al Bristol Britannia flight crew,
  96–97, 102–104, 165, 168, 188
Blanc, Shimon, 166, 179
Eichmann disguised as, 168–169
Hassin, Gady, 164, 166, 184
Klein, Yosef, 102–105, 111, 116–117,
  149–152, 167, 168, 170, 173–174,
  177–178, 181
"monkey business crews," 154
Peleg, Adi, 96–97, 150, 170–172, 178
Shaul, Shaul, 164, 166, 175–180, 182,
  184
Shimoni, Yehuda, 89, 102–103,
  102–105, 105, 155, 165
Tirosh, Barcuh, 96–97
Tohar, Zvi, 96–97, 96 (picture),

155–156, 163–166, 172–180,
  182–183, 188
Wedeles, Shmuel, 155, 162–163, 166,
  170–171, 178
Elian, Yonah, 114 (picture)
in capture operation, 83, 87–90,
  114–115, 118
exam of Eichmann after capture,
  135–136, 167
sedation of Eichmann, 169–170, 169
  (picture), 172–173, 180, 184
extradition processes, 39, 48, 49, 87

F
Final Solution
Eichmann charged with genocide
  for, 191–192, 191 (picture), 199
Eichmann's denial of involvement in,
  79, 81, 148–149, 157–161
Eichmann's work toward, 3–6,
  12–16, 22–23
extermination as, 13–16
Jewish resettlement vs., 12, 149,
  157–158
stages of outlined, 5–6
forged documents and passports
for capture operation agents, 82, 84
  (picture), 111–113, 133
Dani as expert making, 93, 111–113,
  152–153, 153 (picture), 167
for "Zeev Zichroni," 152–153, 153
  (picture), 167, 171 (picture)
Fuldner, Carlos, 78, 145–146

G
Gat, Yaakov (capture operation agent),
  85 (picture), 91, 193
in capture operation, 83, 87, 89, 91,
  92, 94–95, 98–99, 105, 118–122,
  128–134, 141–142, 162
with Eichmann in Israel, 188
surveillance of Eichmann by 94–95,
  98–99
See also capture operation; capture
  operation agents
genocide, 13, 22, 88, 121, 195, 215
See also concentration camps
Germany, 12, 13, 19, 39, 48, 49,
  50–53, 52–53 (picture)
ghettos, Jewish, 6–7, 7 (picture), 9,
  10, 19, 202
Goren, Yoel, 40, 45, 169–170,
  172–173

H
Harel, Isser (head of the Mossad),
  36–38, 38 (picture)

Harel, Isser (head of the Mossad)
(*continued*)
on Bauer and claims about
Eichmann, 39–40, 41, 46–48
bringing Eichmann to Ben-Gurion,
188–190
in capture operation, 68–69, 81–83,
86–90, 99–101, 115–120, 126,
151–152, 151–153
on capturing Eichmann alive, 51,
68–69
on interrogation of Eichmann,
139–140, 144
reports to, 39–45, 47, 66, 68, 74,
192–193
See also capture operation; capture
operation agents
Hausner, Gideon (prosecutor), 201,
204
Heninger, Otto (Adolf Eichmann), 76,
137, 143
Hermann, Lothar, 29–30, 29 (picture),
42
communication with Bauer, 30–31,
33, 35 (pictures)
on Eichmann in Argentina, 30–35,
40–45
meeting "Nick" Eichmann, 28–30
reward from Israel for, 214
Hermann, Sylvia, 33, 33 (picture), 214
relationship with "Nick" Eichmann,
28–30, 32, 143
surveillance and identification of
Eichmann by, 33, 34, 42–44, 55,
143, 227 (Ch. 2 notes)
Hitler, Adolf. *See* anti-Semitism; Final
Solution; Nazis
Hofstetter, Ephraim (Karl Huppert),
41–44
Holocaust survivors
experiences of, 6–10, 16–19, 29, 31,
41, 88, 91, 103, 112, 121, 194
(picture), 204, 210
experiences of, reluctance to talk,
38–39
speaking out after Eichmann trial,
194 (picture)
testimony about at Eichmann's trial,
201–204
as witnesses to Eichmann's
execution, 210

I
Ilani, Ephraim (capture operation
agent), 41–42, 45, 83
in capture operation, 83, 87–91, 104,
111

on plan to get Eichmann to Israel,
140
surveillance of Eichmann, 95
See also capture operation; capture
operation agents
Israel, 26, 37, 39
Arab Legion *vs.*, 26, 37–38
on finding Eichmann, initial
response to, 28, 39–40
relations with Argentina, 196–198
See Ben-Gurion, David; Eichmann
(Adolf), in Israel
Israeli paramilitary organizations, 37,
155

J
"Jewish question." *See* Final Solution
Jewish resettlement, ideas about, 12,
149, 157–158

K
Klement, Ricardo (Adolf Eichmann),
48–50, 54–66, 64–65 (picture),
77–78, 78 (picture), 118–119,
122–123, 137–138, 143
See also Eichmann (Adolf), in
Argentina
Knesset, 51, 190, 192

L
Landau, Moshe, 199, 205, 206 (picture)
license plates, fake, 112–113, 113
(picture), 134, 167, 172

M
Malkin, Fruma, 88, 121, 195, 215–217,
216–217 (picture)
Malkin, Peter (capture operation
agent), 85 (picture), 88, 121,
214–215
artwork by, 152, 158–159 (picture),
216–217 (picture)
in capture operation, 83, 87–90, 104,
106–107, 113–118, 121–122,
128–135, 136, 141–142, 147–149,
152, 157–161, 169
interrogation of Eichmann by,
147–149, 157–162
on silence and secrecy of mission,
193, 195, 214–215
See also capture operation; capture
operation agents
Medad, Yaakov (capture operation
agent), 83, 85 (picture), 101, 119,
134, 141–142, 162
See also capture operation; capture
operation agents

Mercedes-Benz company (Buenos Aires), 122–123, 146
Mossad, 36–38
    file on Eichmann, 28, 54, 66, 88, 136 (picture)
    See also capture operation; capture operation agents
Munkács ghetto, 6–7, 7 (picture), 9, 19, 202

N

Nazis
    Argentine government welcoming, 27–28
    Eichmann as leader for, 3–6
    Gestapo, 12
    Heydrich, Reinhard, 12–13
    Himmler, Heinrich, 15–16, 20
    Kristallnacht, 29, 50
    post-trial arrest of, 213–214
    Mengele, Josef, 166
    safe houses for in Europe, 77
    SD Nazi intelligence service, 11
    SS (Schutzstaffel), 3–4, 11, 12 (picture), 13, 22
    See also Eichmann (Adolf); Final Solution
neo-Nazism
    in Argentina, 28, 68, 146–147, 147 (picture), 197, 213–214
    in Germany, 50–51
    Tacuara, 146–147, 156, 197

O

Office of Strategic Services (OSS), 21–23

S

safe houses, 76
    Doron, 105, 112–115
    Maoz, 98, 101, 110–111, 167
    for Nazis in Europe, 77
    searching for in Buenos Aires, 104–105
    See also Tira safe house
Sapir, Zeev
    Holocaust experiences of, 6–10, 16–19, 202, 204
    testimony in Eichmann trial, 200–204, 203 (picture)
sayanim, 54–63, 72–73, 140
Schmidt, Francisco (Adolf Eichmann), 44–45
Senegal, 97, 156, 163, 165–166, 175, 179–184
Shai intelligence services, 37–38
Shalom, Avraham (capture operation agent), 81–82, 84 (picture)

in capture operation, 82–83, 89–90, 93–94, 112–113, 114–115, 118, 121–122, 128–135, 136–140
    reaction to Eichmann capture announcement, 192–193
    surveillance of Eichmann by, 98–99, 106–107
    See also capture operation; capture operation agents
Shin Bet, 38, 47, 66–68, 81, 82, 94, 137, 154, 188, 195
    See also capture operation; capture operation agents
surveillance activities
    cars used for, 54, 58–72, 70 (picture), 106
    by Hermann family, 31–35, 42–45, 55, 143, 228 (Ch. 2 notes)
    by Mossad agents, 54–63, 63–66, 64–65 (picture), 69–74, 73 (picture), 94–95, 98–99, 106–110, 108–109 (picture)

T

Tabor, Moshe (capture operation agent), 85 (picture), 87–88, 152
    in capture operation, 82–83, 87–90, 104, 112–114, 117–118, 121–122, 128–134, 141–142, 152
    escorting Eichmann in Israel, 188
    on silence and secrecy of mission, 193
    See also capture operation; capture operation agents
Tacuara, 146–147, 156, 197
tattoos, 16, 194 (picture), 204, 210
Tira safe house, 105–106, 115
    agents' mood and duties at, 151–153
    Eichmann's captivity at, 117, 132, 134–144
    See also capture operation; Eichmann (Adolf), capture of

W

Wiesenthal, Simon (Nazi hunter), 21–23, 22 (picture), 25–28, 214

Z

Zichroni, Zeev (Adolf Eichmann), 152–153, 153 (picture), 167, 171 (picture)
Zionism, 37, 189
    See also Israel; Palestine

Nazi-occupied Norway, February 27, 1943

In a staggered line, they cut across the mountain on their skis. Dressed in white camouflage suits over British Army uniforms, the young men threaded through the stands of pine and moved down the sharp, uneven ground. The silence was broken only by the swoosh of skis and the occasional slap of a pole against a branch. The warm, steady wind that blew through Vestfjord Valley dampened even these sounds. This was the same wind that would eventually, hopefully, blow their tracks away.

A mile into their trek, the woods became too dense and steep to descend by any means other than by foot. The nine Norwegian commandos took off their skis and balanced them on their shoulders. Then they slid and trudged down through the wet and heavy snow. They carried thirty-five-pound backpacks filled with survival gear, submachine guns, grenades, pistols, explosives, and knives. Each one also had a cyanide pill in case of capture by the enemy. Often the weight of their equipment made them sink to their waists in the snow.

Suddenly, the forest cleared, and they came upon the road. Ahead of them, on the other side of a terrifying gorge, stood Vemork, their target. The enormous power station, and the eight-story hydrogen plant in front of it, were built on a rocky shelf that extended over the gorge. Below it, the Måna River snaked through a valley so deep that the sun rarely reached its base.

Despite the distance across the gorge, and the wind singing in their ears, the commandos could hear the station's low hum.

Before Hitler invaded Norway and the Germans seized control of the plant, Vemork would have been lit up like a beacon. But now its windows were blacked out to discourage nighttime raids from Allied bombers. High on the icy crag, its dark silhouette looked like a winter fortress. A single-lane suspension bridge provided the only point of entry for workers and vehicles, and it was closely guarded by the Nazis. Mines littered the surrounding hillsides. Patrols swept the grounds. Searchlights, sirens, machine-gun nests, and a barrack of troops were also at the ready.

And now the commandos were going to break into it.

The young men stood mesmerized. They had been told the plant produced something called "heavy water," and with this mysterious substance, the Nazis would be able "to blow up a good part of London." But none of the saboteurs were there for heavy water, or for London. They had seen their country invaded by the Germans, their friends killed and humiliated, their families starved, their rights curtailed. They were there for Norway, for the freedom of its lands and people from Nazi rule.

They refastened their skis and started down the road to their mission.

German forces attack Norway in April 1940.

CHAPTER 01

INVASION

In the dark early hours of April 9, 1940, a fierce wind swept across the decks of the German cruiser *Hipper* and the four destroyers at its stern as they cut into the fjord toward Trondheim, Norway. The ships approached the three forts guarding the entrance to the city, all crews at the ready. A Norwegian patrol signaled for the boats to identify themselves. In English, the *Hipper*'s captain returned that they were a British ship with orders to "go towards Trondheim. No unfriendly intentions." As the patrol shone a spotlight across the water, it was blinded by searchlights from the *Hipper*, which suddenly sped up and blew smoke to hide its whereabouts.

Signals and warning rockets lit up the night. Inside the Norwegian forts, alarms rang and orders were given to fire on the invading ships. But the inexperienced Norwegian soldiers struggled to shoot their guns. By the time they were prepared, the *Hipper* was already steaming past the first fort. At the second fort, the bugler who should have sounded the alarm had fallen asleep at his post. The moment the gunners there opened fire, their searchlights malfunctioned, so they could not see their targets.

At 4:25 A.M., the German force set anchor in Trondheim's harbor. Cutters began bringing hundreds of soldiers from the warships to the shore. The soldiers spread out from the port into the defenseless streets. The Nazi invasion of Norway had begun.

●●●

In a large hall at the Norwegian Institute of Technology (NTH), twenty minutes away from Trondheim's harbor, Leif Tronstad gathered his fellow teachers, their students, and a handful of others. Word of the invasion had reached him before the break of day, and while his wife and children slept, he had rushed to the Institute. From the few reports he and others had received, all of Norway looked to be under attack. Most major cities had fallen alongside Trondheim, but the capital, Oslo, was rumored to be holding out.

The group debated what they should do. One among them, a firebrand named Knut Haukelid, who was visiting friends in the city, wanted to fight with whatever weapons they could find. The Germans were invading their country, and they must resist. Others preached caution. They did not know exactly what Hitler intended for Norway, and their small country, with its limited military, stood little chance against German might.

When Tronstad spoke, he held everyone's attention. At thirty-seven years of age, he was the university's youngest full professor, and a favorite in its classrooms. Of medium height, he had blue eyes and ash-blond hair parted neatly on the side, with a light dance of crow's feet around his eyes.

He told those assembled that he would travel to Oslo, where, as a reserve officer in the Army, he had standing orders to go once war broke out. He suggested those with military experience should do the same. As for the others, he said, each man needed to follow his own conscience on what action he should take, but all must remember their country was in desperate need. "Whatever you do," he said, "your actions will be history in a hundred years." With that, he said his goodbyes.

Tronstad had feared this would happen — that Norway would be attacked and its "sleeping government" would leave the country unprepared to mount a defense. Since the day Adolf Hitler had invaded Poland in September 1939, and Britain's soon-to-be prime minister Winston Churchill had announced, "We are fighting to save the whole world from the pestilence of Nazi tyranny," it was clear to Tronstad that Norway would not be allowed to maintain the neutral stand it had held in the First World War. The fight between the Allies and the Nazis in mainland Europe had stalled, and the two sides had circled around Norway for months. With its rich natural resources and strategic position in the North Sea, Tronstad's homeland was too good a prize to leave unclaimed.

As Tronstad hurried home, German soldiers occupied the city around him, marching in columns through the streets. They established machine-gun nests and mortar positions at key spots throughout the city, and called out warnings in German not to resist. Tronstad ignored them. When he reached his two-story house on the city's outskirts, he told his wife, Bassa, that they were not safe in Trondheim. He would take her and the children to a mountain tourist lodge 100 miles to the south, then he would go to Oslo to join the Army.

Together, they woke up their young children, Sidsel and Leif, and helped them dress and pack. Fifteen minutes later, they piled into their car. As they headed south over a river bridge, two ash-colored bombers flew overhead.

"What kind of plane is that?" Sidsel asked.

"It is a German plane," Tronstad said, his first explanation of their hurried departure. "I'm afraid the war's come to our country."

German police troops march into Oslo in May 1940.

•••

Twenty-eight-year-old Knut Haukelid chose a different path out of Trondheim. He and a few NTH students took control of a freight train in the city and drove it almost halfway to Oslo, until they found the tracks closed. They abandoned the train and took a bus to the nearest Army headquarters. There, they learned the heartbreaking news that the Nazis had taken Oslo, and King Haakon VII and the Norwegian government had fled the capital.

In fighting to free his country, Haukelid found his purpose. He tracked down a regiment battling the Germans and received a Krag rifle and thirty rounds of ammunition. At first glance, Haukelid probably looked similar to all the other soldiers the commander was sending into war, with nothing particularly notable about him. He had fair hair, blue eyes, and a medium build that hunched slightly at the shoulders, and at five foot ten, he was just above average height.

Yet over the next three weeks, despite having no military experience, Haukelid fought ferociously for his country and king, refusing to surrender as their invaders demanded. His battalion ambushed a line of German tanks at a mountain pass, wiping them out with homemade bombs and a single cannon, but apart from that one success, they were pushed back again and again. The German *Blitzkrieg*, with its armored vehicles, fast bombers, and well-trained troops, were simply too overwhelming a force to resist.

His regiment surrendered, but Haukelid did not. He tried to reach the fighting in the two strategic valleys that ran between Oslo and Trondheim, but his countrymen were already in retreat. Finally, he traveled into the capital and went to his parents'

Knut Haukelid.

home, a spacious apartment in the city center. His father was away, so only his mother was there to welcome him. Haukelid went into the room where he still kept a few possessions and closed the door. "What are you doing?" his mother asked.

"Getting some things," Haukelid said, grabbing his cross-country skis and boots from the closet.

"You need to get out and fight," she told him.

That was exactly his plan.

Before the war came, Knut Haukelid was a bit of a lost soul. He was born in Brooklyn, New York, to Norwegian immigrants, but his family returned to Oslo when he and his twin sister, Sigrid, were only toddlers. Dyslexic and restless, he hated school. Sitting still in those hard chairs all day, listening to the drone of teachers, was torture for him. Talking in class only turned the screws, thanks to a slight stutter. He entertained himself by pulling pranks. Once, he released a snake in the middle of class, earning one of his many suspensions.

The lone place Haukelid was able to run free was the family's country lodge. On weekends and in summertime, he skied, fished, camped, and hunted with his grandfather in the mountains and lakes of Telemark, west of Oslo. Haukelid was told the old tales of trolls inhabiting and protecting the lands of Norway, and he believed them. His faith in these creatures lent even more magic to the woods he loved.

After high school, Haukelid left for the United States to attend college. He traveled the country, working at farms for spare cash. A few years later, he came back to Norway. His father found him a well-paid job at Oslo's biggest bank, but Haukelid turned it down. He could earn more money, he told his father, fishing for trout — and off he went. After several months of fishing, he moved again, this time to Berlin. (His sister, Sigrid, left the country as well; she went to Hollywood and became a movie star known as the "siren of the fjords.") Haukelid studied engineering, learned German, and questioned his future. In 1936, he saw Hitler's propaganda parade at the Olympics. One night, when he ran into a drunk Nazi Party member who was spouting one nasty statement after another, he dropped him with a punch.

At last, he returned again to Oslo, and finally gave in to his father's wish for him to get serious with his career and his life. He took a job with his father's firm, importing engineering equipment from the United States, and he fell in love with a young woman named Bodil, a physical therapist who treated him for some back pain from all his outdoor adventures. Still, Haukelid was restless, not quite at peace with himself, until he found his purpose in defending his country.

• • •

Despite the heroic efforts of many Norwegians like Haukelid, by early June 1940, Hitler controlled the entire country. King Haakon and the government fled to England by ship, and the nation's top general pleaded to his former soldiers, "Remain true and prepared" for the future fight.

Haukelid got straight to it. In Oslo, he and a friend who had received wireless training in Britain launched their own spy network for the Allies. For months, the two moved from hut to hut in the woods outside Oslo, sending radio signals to Allied forces but hearing nothing in return. Through a range of contacts in the city, they collected intelligence on the German command in the capital — everyone from Reichskommissar Josef Terboven, who served as Hitler's right hand in Norway, to General Nikolaus von Falkenhorst, who oversaw the German military forces, to SS Lieutenant Colonel Heinrich Fehlis, who ran the security services. Unable to make contact with British or Norwegian allies in London, they continued their efforts nevertheless, and even hatched a plot to kidnap Vidkun Quisling, the Norwegian fascist whose political party served as a puppet government for Terboven. Haukelid and his friend were daring and brave; they were also amateurish and terribly ineffective. But they had joined a growing resistance movement that hoped to drive the Nazis from their land. They all felt they had to do *something*.

Reichskommissar Terboven moved quickly to consolidate Nazi rule. He removed any Norwegians not loyal to the "New Order" from positions of influence: judges, clergy, journalists, business heads, policemen, mayors, and teachers alike. The

SS Lieutenant Colonel Heinrich Fehlis and Reichskommissar Josef Terboven.

Norwegian parliament was closed permanently, its members sent home. The main government buildings in the heart of Oslo flew Nazi flags.

The Nazis' presence extended well beyond Oslo. Travel after curfew or beyond a certain place without an identity card or pass was made illegal. Radios were banned. Anyone breaking the rules was subject to arrest — or whatever punishment the Nazis chose, since it was the Nazis, not the police, who enforced the law. Nothing was published in Norway without the censor's stamp of approval. New schoolbooks were printed to teach students that Hitler was Norway's savior. Strict rationing of coal, gas, food, milk, and clothing left families scraping by. People found themselves making shoes from fish skins and clothes from old newspaper. All the while, the Germans took whatever they

Nazi flags hang in the central Oslo train station.

wanted for themselves, from the finest cuts of meat to the best houses.

Some Norwegians supported the new German order. Many others merely did what they were told. But there were others still who pushed back against the Nazis. In September 1941, workers throughout Oslo went on strike against the strict rationing of milk. Terboven put martial law into effect. Hundreds were arrested, and the security chief, Fehlis, ordered the execution of the two strike leaders. Following this, the Nazi secret police, the Gestapo, intensified their hunt for underground resistance cells.

Soon they came for Haukelid, storming his family's apartment. He was not home, but the Gestapo arrested his mother, Sigrid, and his new wife, Bodil. When asked where her son was, Sigrid slapped the Gestapo officer in the face and said, "He's in the mountains."

"No," the Nazi said. "He's in England. Our contact tells us he's already been taken across the North Sea. And what do you think he is doing there?"

"You will find out when he comes back!" she promised.

• • •

Leif Tronstad would not stand for the Nazis living in his country and lording power over its people. Their presence was a violation of everything he held dear, and their occupation robbed him of the life he'd built from nothing.

Three months before Tronstad was born, his father died of a heart attack. His mother supported her four sons by serving as a maid at private dinner parties hosted by the wealthier families in their neighborhood outside Oslo. Growing up, Leif was either studying, running, or working. He excelled at all three activities, setting new track records and making the highest marks at school. His favorite subject was always science. He simply liked to understand how the world worked. He graduated college with top honors, married his childhood sweetheart, Bassa, and won scholarships to focus on chemistry at some of the best institutes in the world, including Cambridge University in England and the Kaiser Wilhelm Institute of Chemistry in Berlin.

Talented not just in the lab but also in theoretical work, Tronstad found many opportunities open to him. Since his first student days, he had wondered whether he should work in industry or teach. In the end, he told Bassa that, while he wanted to be a professor, he would leave the decision to her. "If you like, I can make as much money as you want," he said. She gave him her blessing to teach. He was soon a professor at NTH. He bought a nice house a ten-minute walk from the university and a car to drive out to his mountain cabin, where he, Bassa, and their two children skied and hiked. During these prewar years, Tronstad also worked as a consultant to several Norwegian companies, advising them on the manufacture of steel, rubber, nitrogen, aluminum, and other industrial products.

After his government surrendered to the Germans, Tronstad returned to Trondheim with his family. He kept his job, but NTH was now under German control. Professors who pledged their allegiance to the Nazis quickly gained power within the university, not to mention board seats on many of the companies where Tronstad consulted. The Nazis intended to use every sector of Norwegian industry to supply its war machine.

Tronstad wanted nothing to do with such efforts. Instead, like Haukelid, he became deeply involved in the underground —

Leif Tronstad.

the homegrown military resistance called Milorg. Through his rich trove of contacts (and by maintaining some of his consulting jobs), he helped supply industrial intelligence to the British. With most of Europe quickly falling under German rule, and the United States not yet in the war, free Britain was the lone beacon of hope for those who wanted to fight the Germans.

In early September 1941, as the Gestapo was breaking up resistance networks across Norway, Tronstad decided to inform the British of a very disturbing development at a place called Vemork. What was happening there could well give the Nazis the power to win the war.

Author photo by Jillian McAlley

Neal Bascomb is the author of six nonfiction books for adults on subjects ranging from a 1905 Russian submarine mutiny to a contemporary high school robotics team. *The Perfect Mile* and *Hunting Eichmann* went on to be *New York Times* and international bestsellers. His first book for young adults, *The Nazi Hunters*, won the YALSA Excellence in Nonfiction Award in 2014, and his second, *Sabotage*, was called "excellent" in a starred review from *School Library Journal*. Neal lives in Seattle with his family. Please visit his website at www .nealbascomb.com and follow him on Twitter at @nealbascomb.

EXPLORE MORE THRILLIN NON-FICTION STORIES FROM NEAL BASCOMB

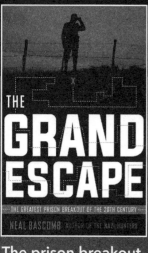

The prison breakout of the century!

"Riveting."

–Susan Campbell Bartoletti, Newbery Honor-winning author of *Hitler Youth: Growing Up in Hitler's Shadow*

"Exciting."

–Steve Sheinkin, Newbery Honor-winnin author of *Bomb: The Race to Build—and Steal—the World's Mos Dangerous Weapon*